AUTOBIOGRAPHY OF KALKI

Ram H. Peswani

First Published in May 2023

ISBN: 978-93-5741-558-3

BLUEROSE PUBLISHERS

www.BlueRoseONE.com

info@bluerosepublishers.com

+91 8882 898 898

Cover Design:

Muskan Sachdeva

Typographic Design:

Hemlata

Distributed by: BlueRose, Amazon, Flipkart

Foreword

(By Swami Brahmachariji)

|| ॐ गं गणपतये नमः ||

My first introduction to respectable Shri Ram Peswaniji was on 2nd May 1993, during his Gangotri Sadhana trip. This trip was totally unplanned. At that time he was doing meditation through which he was guided by his Inner Voice.

Shri Peswaniji mentioned that as per Lotus Sutra, he was observing his body parts during meditation and cleansing his physical and mental well-being step by step.

His family was not in favor of him doing his Sadhana practice by staying in jungles or any retreat. Through his Sadhana he normalized his bad Cholesterol, B.P., Sugar, and all other health problems. At that time his physical state was undergoing this AUTOMATIC NATURAL PROCESS, through which he would observe his painful point, and gradually after a few days, it would heal. Then this process would automatically move on towards the next painful point.

Respectable Shri Peswaniji mentioned that he had attended a camp at Nashik Vipassana Centre hence it was easy for him to do this Sadhana.

During one of my visits to Pune, he gave me a book, 'The Lotus Sutra' which has teachings of Gautam Buddha. Ram Peswaniji mentioned that the teachings and content of 'The Lotus Sutra' matched completely with his feelings and experiences, and with the scriptures which he read, and understood through the Veda- Upanishads, When he explained some of the contents I felt that all his experiences are the same as those mentioned in Vedic scriptures.

As I understood, Shri Peswaniji was in search of the right path he must choose to find answers to his questions. With this objective in mind, we traveled together to many places in the country.

Over the years Shri Peswaniji has supported us financially. He offered to donate his Maruti Van to our Chamba Ashram even though we did not require it. Finally, I agreed and in April 1999, it was handed over to Chamba Ashram. Although it was a used car, we had driven it to Delhi, Haridwar, Indore, Nashik, Pune, Mumbai, Surat, Ahmedabad, Mt. Abu, Ajmer, Jaipur, Delhi, Haryana, Punjab, Jammu and many more places.

During winters he used to visit me and we would drive in his car in search of the right path. Till date, he has visited Chamba three times. His meditation experiences are quite novel and super spiritual. It is a matter of pride to us that he has reached this state and it motivates us too.

I remember, long back he mentioned that he had gone to Balaji's Durbar at Tirupati and prayed. Soon after the visit, he felt substantial improvement in his health and financial matters. During one such trip, we drove from Pune to Ganga Sagar, Bengal by road and returned via Delhi. We visited Nashik, Aurangabad, Shegaon, Rajkot, Sambalpur, Cuttack, Kharagpur, Calcutta, Gangasagar, Vardhaman, Bodhgaya, Kashi - Banaras, Allahabad, Kanpur, and Delhi. We stayed in Ashrams at various places. This trip was a very pleasant and easy-going experience for us. Our objective was clear – we wanted to find the Truth and follow the right Path to progress further in meditation.

We talked about every spiritual aspect of our life and I saw Ram as a transparent, kind, loving, and affectionate person.

I accept Shri Peswaniji as a Guru and a person who can show the path to many lost souls. I feel blessed to have met such an affectionate person.

Once again in August 2006, Shri Peswaniji and I took an impromptu trip from Pune to Leh Ladakh by road in his car. We both took turns in driving while the other rested.

We started from Pune and enroute covered Nashik, Traimbakeshwar, Ganganagar, Bathinda, Chamba, Dharamashala, Manali, Rohtang pass, Lahaul Spiti and reached Leh Ladakh. We stayed there for 5 days in a hotel and saw the local area.

On our way back, we went to the Ashram of the Demon Master with whom Peswaniji had a sad experience, but we could not meet that Master.

Peswaniji has many relatives in Delhi including his daughter Renu. I returned from Delhi to Chamba while he proceeded to Pune. It was a good experience.

Shri Peswaniji mentioned a few times about this Master who with the help of his sister, used to send subtle energies to attract groups of devotees. This Master used negative energies against Shri Peswaniji and his family too, which troubled him over the years mentally & physically. Shri Peswaniji has assured that this Autobiography will give detailed information about his relentless effort for around 15 years to trace the lost soul, and the present status. It looks like Peswaniji's Godly powers, and Karmas continued to save him till he reached a state where he learned to dissolve such evil powers.

Following the death of the Demon Master on 30th June 2022, Shri Peswaniji has been released completely from the influence of his evilness which he could see through his meditation energies as these were unobstructed and clear.

Now, I am confident that Peswaniji can help the Universe without any hurdle from the subtle negative energies that had obstructed him and as the Universe now flows through him and he dissolves the negativity, I pray that he attains his future goals quickly.

All The Best.

Thank you

M.R. Brahmachari

Acknowledgments

Writing a book about my spiritual life was more challenging than I had anticipated and more rewarding than I could have ever imagined. Many people have made it possible for me to write this book, and I would like to acknowledge and extend my sincere gratitude.

First of all, I would like to thank and seek the blessings of all the Gurus, God and Avatars, who came into my life to make this life experience a Spiritual evolvement for me.

I would like to remember my grandparents and parents with regard and honor. I will forever be grateful for the knowledge and values they have instilled in me. I would like to mention my wife, Smt Savitri Peswani, for her unwavering belief in me during all my struggles and successes. I am eternally grateful to my son, Sunil Peswani, daughters Sonia Chandiramani & Renu Bathija, and my late loving daughter Gita/ Upasana Matnani for motivating me to capture my Spiritual life in this book. They have all helped, motivated, and transcribed my thoughts into this book based on my Audio tapes.

I am grateful to Swami Brahmchariji for penning the foreword for this book. Thank you, Swamiji, for letting me know that you have great memories of me.

I would like to extend my heartfelt gratitude to my age-old friend and well-wisher G.Prasad Aminji for assisting me in my work.

My most sincere thanks to all my extended family and friends for their heartfelt support, ready smiles, shared meals, advice, perspectives, friendship, and wandering the meandering path of life with me. Thank you to all the individuals I had the opportunity to lead, to be led by, or to observe their leadership from afar and draw inspiration from.

I am immensely indebted to Ms Leena Prabhu for her editorial help, keen insight, and breathing life into my stories.

Finally, I would like to thank you, my cherished readers. To get my story told gives me immense satisfaction, and to have it received by you, feels surreal. I hope you enjoy reading this book- *Autobiography of Kalki.* Initially this book was named as *The Transition- Buddha to Kalki,* as my spiritual evolvement from Buddha teachings finally gave me wings to fly with a shining Sword to reach the pinnacles of evolution of the final Avatar. Later on we changed the name to AUTOBIOGRAPHY OF KALKI.

Ram H. Peswani

Contents

Introduction

The message of the Book

Ram Peswani with the book of Lotus Sutra in hand. Kalki, in the form of a star, enters the body of Ram Peswani to drink the evil poison of earth and to usher in heaven.

Kalki, riding a flying horse with a sword in hand, slaying evilness[1]

Kalki avatar is mentioned in many Hindu texts, including but not limited to the Mahabharata, Vishnu Purana, Matsya Purana, Bhavishya Purana, Kalki Purana, and Bhagavata Purana.

A journey that started on 2nd August 1937 in Sindh, has continued for over eighty-five years. Wandering across the globe, touching lives, and pursuing careers gave me enriching experiences and unforgettable

1 Courtesy: Kalki Avatar (refer Appendix pg II)

spiritual encounters. This journey has been nothing less than a blessing.

As God continues to sketch my journey, I wish to pause for a moment to reflect on where He has brought me and what He has brought me through. I have always nurtured a deep desire to share snippets of my spiritual journey with those dear to me and the world at large. While I still have plenty to explore, this book is a sincere attempt to trace my wanderings through life and the world inside.

The book also aims to quench the thirst of the many itinerant souls who genuinely want to understand the Lotus Sutra and the role that the next Avatar (Kalki) plays. Lotus Sutra describes a fantastic world of the Buddha's mind of enlightenment - beyond Time and Space. Music resounding from the depth of galaxies, Kinnara Gods with beautiful voices, mountains of gold, trees with jewels, flowers raining from the sky, and many thousands of Bodhisattvas living in harmony with the Buddha, their Guru. This fantastic world with its dream-like environment can only be described through poetry. I have endeavored to offer insights into this holy book by Buddha. I immensely owe to Burton Watson for translating the Lotus Sutra into English. I refer to it for guidance. It is like a Holy Bible to me. The base of my book lies in Lotus Sutra.

I have gone through each line of Lotus Sutra and practically learnt it after contemplating each verse for days or months together using my inner guidance. I have written many statements in this book with reference to Lotus Sutra, sometimes mentioning the actual page number and sometimes as a passing reference.

Many people that I have met on Internet forums, could not even understand the book of Lotus Sutra. Many books have been written on Sri Ram (Sri Ramcharitrmanas), Lord Krishna (Bhagwad Gita), but few on Buddha and Lotus Sutra and almost none on Kalki. As a result of my 30 years of asceticism, I went through the inward journey to understand it. Readers, if interested, can read the book to understand in depth, or can contact me, wherever I have mentioned Lotus Sutra.

Autobiography of Kalki, apart from being a documentation of my personal and professional life lived so far, also features candid assessments of living my life as per the teachings from Lotus Sutra, abiding by it, and practically experiencing it. I will be honest to say I have understood 60% of it. Having lived through near-death experiences and dissolving endless miseries of Spirits and souls, I have exerted myself to offer the reader a unique, first-hand perspective of my visits to different Planes of Existence and to convey a strong sense of what an inner war is like and how it led me to the role of Kalki.

I have met four different Gurus in my life of spirituality. First was the Star, who entered my body in 1951. He is a son of God. He comes from planes 0 to 15.

He has been with me since 1951 which I was not aware of then. From 1951 till 30th June 1992, the contact was only one-sided. The Star was guiding my life. Second Guru was Narayana - my Tirupati Guru. He guided me since 1970 and was with me up to 1994. Narayana handed me to the third Guru- Buddha, who taught me The Lotus Sutra. The fourth Guru was Ghost Guru in 1995, through whom I learned about the Dark World. The Inner Star Guru still guides me.

Some may find the content controversial as they may have never dealt with issues which disturb our instilled values in life, but these kinds of things often happen in life. The book is an account straight from my heart. In the pursuit of following the course of my life's journey, equal emphasis has been laid on my personal experiences vis-a-vis my family, deep bonds, attachment, cleansing, dissolving of negativity, first inside and then the whole Universe as my large family.

~Ram. H .Peswani

Chapter 1

"No man can win every battle,

but no man should fall without a struggle." [2]

AUTOBIOGRAPHY OF KALKI, is connected with the tenth Avatar on Earth, which now resides in the 26th plane. I am one of the sons of God. I live in the upper plane number 5, as a Son of God and come down to lower levels to extend the Creation.

Initially I had come down to the Earth i.e. 26th plane along with the Lotus Sutra of Buddha system some billions of years ago.

Gods & Vedas

Planes of Existence

I believe in God, Vedas and Sanatan Dharma. Let me first talk about God and how and what I understand about HIM. To start with, the Universe had only God, nothing else. There was no Space, Time, Creation, Stars, or life. There was nothing else other than God.

So, as per my understanding, God first created this creation out of His body and Himself. He is infinite. So,

---

2 Courtesy: by PeterParker https://medium.com/@Sanskriti_Sinha/no-man-can-win-every-battle-but-no-man-should-fall-without-a-struggle-peter-parker-1286b2feba7a

God is everywhere in the space of experience and He is in the form of awareness. God could divide himself. He created a separate entity from a portion of His existence. This separate entity, the son of God, stays in a different Plane of Existence from that of God. Even after creating scores of such sons, God is infinite, as per the Sanathan Dharma[3]. His sons acquire some skills in each of their existence. Skills in various planes are different. When I went deeper into my meditation, I got the knowledge of various 'Planes of Existence'. These Planes of Existence will become very important as we proceed further, and it is better to understand these in depth.

God is everywhere and He is in the form of awareness. We, as human beings, can perceive him by awareness in our bodies. If we want to know about God or wish to feel Him, we have to be in the state of awareness. God is pure awareness and a fraction of Him is present not only in our body but in every body, every life, everywhere.

So first was God, who was the pure awareness, at plane 0 (zero). His fractions were his sons. They were in possession of particular skills and could further subdivide. More and more sons were created, and these sons went on different planes. By the time they went down to the 15th plane, this awareness of God had become minuscule, with some level of skills.

---

3 Courtesy: The Concept of Infinity in Sanatan Dharma (ref Appendix pg xii)

The awareness was maximum in plane number Zero, but at each lower plane, awareness kept on reducing. In plane 15, awareness got reduced to a low level. These 15 planes of existence were created during the initial process of God's experiment of dividing and creating a variety out of Himself.

A point to note in this whole process is that God, who is at Level Zero, could withdraw all these creations back to Himself anytime. Awareness below Him in plane number One could also withdraw all the creations below Him by pure awareness, but they could not disturb or withdraw creations of God at the higher planes above them.

In short, God is in plane number Zero. He has created his sons who settled in plane number 1 and 2. He can withdraw all of them into Himself. We will refer to them as Sons of Gods. Each Son of God could subdivide Himself by His awareness, and each one can withdraw his own creations but not the creations of other Sons of Gods.

So, awareness of God is like a breath in our life. When God breathes out, the creation of Sons of Gods occurs, and these Gods settle in different Planes in the Universe. When He breathes in, the whole creation below him goes back to Him, dissolves, or gets absorbed. This is called Mahayug.

There are 16 planes of Gods' Existence. God would initiate a creation which would subdivide further. This would continue from plane 0 to plane 15. Gods in the lower planes could withdraw only their Creation back to them. They could create and they could withdraw only what they had created. In the beginning of each Yug, Sons of Gods initiate the creations and inhale the same just before the end of that Yug.

But things did not stop at that level. God was not happy. He observed that most of the Gods and their sons down the planes were bogged down on the cycle of creations and withdrawal process with not much progress. The process was aimless and there was no systematic development. God had to communicate with lower Gods to create awareness amongst themselves on the reality of the existence of sources of life energy viz., Atmas and Emptiness. Atmas originated from the Gods and the other source of life energy came from Emptiness which was from images of Gods. Images of Gods are not real but they have the properties of the God Himself. These are also called Shunyta, Shadow or Maya. With a clear understanding of Gods' creations and that of Emptiness, the result was encouraging and progressed as desired by God. The creations continued with the Gods and images of Gods, further down to plane number 31. The creations between 16 & 31 were mixed creations of Gods and the images of Gods and had awareness, space and time as well as acquired wisdom and skills of varying degrees.

I believe that Gautam Buddha wrote about the creation of the shadow or image of God as "Emptiness" as it had no existence, it was a mere shadow. At the same time, Sanatan Dharam talks about it as Maya (unreal). All terms, whether Image, Shadow, Maya, unreal or Emptiness, are all one and the same thing.

This explains the Planes of Existence from 0 to 31[4] in simple words.

All my writings henceforth will refer to these Planes of Existence and their importance in our life.

---

4 Note: Total planes are 32 which include plane 0 and 1 to 31 planes.

(Courtesy : https://www.pinterest.com/pin/735705289103270121/)

So, Initially, there was only God and God alone. Then he divided himself into 3 Gods, whom we call Brahma, Vishnu and Maheshwar. Sons of Brahma came into existence, and then Brahma with his sons started the creation downwards.

This creation needed the guidance of Avatars and messengers from time to time.

The Ten Avatars[5]

5 Courtesy: Ten Avatars of Lord Vishnu

(refer Appendix pg xx), Art by Sonali Mohanty,

https://www.facebook.com/SonaliMohantyArt/posts/dashavatara-1-and-230x24acrylicmixed-media-in-stretched-canvas-with-frame-2020-o/1453764878141590/

Our Vedas tell us that this creation evolved over a period of time[6], and Avatars descended from the top, from Heaven down to this creation to help its evolution in the right direction. They tell us that the first avatar was in the form of a *Fish.* Life started on this Earth in the form of a Fish. Life started in the Water.

The second Avatar was a *Tortoise.* This evolution had to move from the Sea to the Land. The tortoise was the one who could live/survive both on the land and in the water.

The third Avatar was a *Boar,* a pig with small legs. He could walk faster than a tortoise on land and looked like an animal.

Puranas and One of the Upanishads attached to the Atharva Veda mentions the fourth Avatar as *Narsimha*[7], a Lion-faced animal with a ferocious look. This allowed him to survive better than other animals.

The fifth Avatar was a short man called *Bauna,* a Vaman Avatar. His forehead was pointed. You can find such people even now. Some of them are typically underdeveloped.

---

6 Courtesy: Vedic Theory of Creation (Refer Appendix pg xxi)

https://www.cs.ubc.ca/~goyal/creation.php

7 Rigveda 1:154 contains a verse which some have interpreted as alluding to the Narasingha Avatar in addition to the Vamana Avatar:One of the Upanishads attached to the Atharva Veda is the Narasingha Tapaniya Upanishad, which not only mentions but describes the Narasimha Avatar in detail.

Sixth was *Parashuram*. He was a man like us but full of emotions, without Wisdom and full of anger.

Seventh was *Rama*. Rama was a family man with full Wisdom about rebirth and karmas, so he created good Karmas towards his parents and the family. He knew that wisdom would create good karmas for him.

The eighth Avatar was *Krishna.* Wisdom advanced to the level where the ruler or the king could give a good life and control many people and families.

The ninth Avatar was *Buddha.* Krishna could travel on a horse or a Chariot for a few thousand kilometers, but Buddha could travel to any part of the Universe at lightning speed through meditation and internal science. If you meditate, you can reach any point in the Universe.

The tenth Avatar is ***Kalki.*** He is shown as a person riding a flying horse with a shining Sword to destroy and eliminate Evil. The Sword in his hand is the *Lotus Sutra- The Sword of Wisdom.* It can slay all the monsters and negative energies like hate, fear, etc. It can also clean up positive energies like *extra/ excess love* because Kalki believes in toning down both misery and happiness.

Kalki with a Sword removes all that is junk, leaving behind only Creativity with Wisdom. Creativity with Wisdom along with its usefulness to everybody else brings evolution to a perfect level. So when Buddha evolves to become Kalki, besides having initial seven chakras, will have three extra energy bodies, which are termed as KAAYAS, namely:

NirmanaKaya, the Creative body shield: Whatever creative work he does, this aura expands. If he does that creative work with wisdom, it becomes DharmaKaya.

DharmaKaya, the Wisdom shield: It can be helpful to a million people or a select few. Depending upon the person's creativity and talent, he gets that much benefit in existence in the form of SambhogaKaya.

SambhogaKaya is the Karma sharing shield.

In this evolution process from *Buddha to Kalki,* Buddha developed three energy bodies, as mentioned above, and later on, as *Kalki,* he got the *Sword of Lotus Sutra.*

The four yugas refer to cosmic ages that are used in the Vedic / Hindu system for measuring universal time. These four ages are known as Satya Yuga, Treta Yuga, Dvapara Yuga, and Kali Yuga. Unlike the Western concept of linear time, Vedic time is cyclical. Like the four seasons of the year, the four ages of a Chaturyuga, or Yuga cycle, rotate without end. A cycle of 4 Yugas is termed as Mahayug. *Kalki is like a machine that processes all life, separates creativity with wisdom from all life, then deposits them in seed form.* Maha Pralay occurs at the end of Maha Yug. *After which, there is another cycle of Yugas.* The Collective Wisdom of all life seeds are deposited and preserved in the Upper Plane. These seeds of creation will sprout faster than the new creation and push the next existence forward. When the creation is perfected, the Star and its guiding Brahma rests. The evolution of each Star ends in rest in Mahapralaya. In this way, all other Stars evolve too. Our Star has selected two-legged human beings as a sample. It will grow as a Milky Way collecting Lights and Stars. The Stars in a Milky Way will dance in the formation like Nataraja. Down each plane, all life will be synchronized to this dance. Life on each plane will be free from Evilness and Suffering.

This book is written to spread the Buddha System and Kalki System. The greatest Wisdom Sutra of Gautam Buddha called Lotus Sutra is hardly known to anyone. Even Buddhists don't understand the book fully.

The problem is that up to Krishna avatar we could write books and read with our senses and mind. But the Lotus Sutra cannot be read through our Senses and minds alone. It has to be understood through Meditation and in meditation, Lotus Sutra begins when we get directly linked with some Higher power who can talk about Lotus Sutra. It has to be experienced internally in our body and mind.

The purpose of this book is to create awareness of Lotus Sutra. Basically each Avatar in Hinduism indicates evolution to higher development. Such as the Avatar from a fish to a tortoise and so on. Each Avatar caused a huge level of evolution. Thus when Buddha Avatar descended on this

Earth, it was far advanced and should have had an equally powerful effect. It has not happened so far but it will happen because the level is so high and so different and so inward that it will take time for people on Earth to understand and assimilate and then its power will be seen.

Chapter 2

"Knowing yourself is the beginning of all Wisdom."
-Aristotle[8]

I am named Ram. In this physical body, I can be compared to a Horse, born on Aug 2, 1937. Assume me to be a Kalki Avatar. Up to the age of 22, i.e., until 1959, this Horse learned to trot, gallop, and walk and knew the intricate roads of life. I could carry the life of co-passengers on my own. Up to the age of 50, I had done well, but in an attempt to be very good to others and the world, I became weak and sick. My shine had diminished. I had lost some beauty. I was also unhappy and started searching for answers. I decided that my body should be energetic, shining, lighter and fit, so that I could fight and try to find a way forward.

At the age of 55 years, in 1992, I thought that meditation could be the way forward to quench my thirst to find answers to my questions.

My mission in life is to cut down the miseries, tone down happiness and stop the negative thoughts in humans; I want to promote selfless approach in human beings so that they can extend their thoughts beyond

---

8 Courtesy: **Aristotle > Quotes https://www.goodreads.com/author/quotes/2192.Aristotle**

themselves and think for all. This way they could realize the Buddha's vision in daily life.

Childhood

I was born as the eldest of five children to Hotchand and Devibai. My father worked in a Telephone Exchange. Although no one in his family was spiritual, over the years, when his mum was widowed, she started visiting Gurdwaras daily. Only his maternal uncle (his mother's brother) was into meditation and had a spiritual inclination.

My Father's name is Hotchand Peswani. My Grandfather, Rijumal Peswani, had four sons and 2 daughters. My Grandfather's sons were: Lalchand, my father Hotchand, was second, then Assandas, and Youngest son, Hundraj. His daughters were: Momtani, who was the eldest and Devi Obraini.

The eldest son, Lalchand had one son named Mohandas.

The second son Hotchand had four sons - Ram Peswani, Manohar Peswani, Laxman Peswani, and one more, who died at the age of 3-4yrs in Sindh, Hyderabad.

I had two sisters Nirmala and Laxmi. Laxmi, my youngest sister and Laxman were born in independent India, the rest of us in Karachi under the protection of our Nana, Gagandas Sabnani. My father used to be a Monitor in Telegraph Exchange. He had passed only

8th, the most educated back then was Assandas, who had passed 10th, and he was employed as Postmaster in the Post Office. Lalchand, who was in Karachi, initially had a big grocery shop, which was a roaring business for him.

Opposite Lalchand's, my *Nana* had a small factory manufacturing wheat flour from wheat. We called it *Chakki.* Maximum education was given to my Uncle-*Maama,* my mother's brother, whose name was Seumal Sabnani. He was the first family member to complete Engineering. The second family member who got highly educated was myself. I did Mechanical Engineering and later on did Higher Education in Electronics & Metallurgy and then Electrical Engineering at Tata's.

My mother's name was Nevi Gagandas Sabnani. Her maiden name was Nevi. After marriage, her name changed to Devibai as per the Hindu tradition. Initially, my mother was like any other girl who loved luxuries, but later on, she changed, and at the end, she was highly religious in the sense that she spent most of the time in Guru Nanak's worship.

At a younger age, she had tried Radha Soami and Nirankaris, but somehow she was not happy with it. My father, Hotchand Peswani, was a worshiper of Shiva. He was a straightforward man, hard-working, and always gave society some service, whatever he could afford. He would work hard at home and then work very sincerely at the office. On his return from the office, he would continue, to carry on with the housework and do odd jobs. I never remembered him demanding anything or asking for anything. He lived a simple life. My mother was also very hard working and took care of all in the family, guiding all on the path of good values. She handled financial matters at home well.

Some crucial incidents in my life:

When I was ten years old, we were in Sindh, and in 1947 India and Pakistan were formed, and we were told that we had to leave this city and go to some place in India. As a child, I saw terrible incidents.

My Grandfather, Nana, an established, very big businessman in Sindh, became a pauper in his final years after moving to Delhi, India. When he was 60, he died an unhappy, depressed man. He lost everything that he had earned through his hard work. He was beaten up when he was in Pakistan. His mother loved the ancestral house and refused to leave the same. My great-grandmother died in shock one night before moving. When my Grandfather went to do her last rites, he was beaten up badly, and it caused a significant scar in his life.

As destined, the whole family left Sindh, now in Pakistan, leaving behind everything they had.

In India, we had to resettle and restart our life from zero. Whatever the compulsion with which those leaders played their games during that time resulted in misery, pain, losses, and death for millions of migrating people, who will never forget and forgive. They should have considered all issues in totality before forming the partition. It was a massive blunder on the part of the politicians.

The second incident took place when I was 14 years old in 1951. I had just passed the 8th class and I was to enter the 9th class. I studied at Ramjas Higher Secondary School in Delhi near my Devnagar House. One Summer night, while I was sleeping outside on the cot in front of my house, looking at the sky, my finger pointed out a Star that came down like a Shooting Star. Strange enough, I felt that something had entered my body at that moment. I now assume it to be Narayana to establish Communication with me.

Until then, I was an average or lower average student in studies, which means I would somehow pass my grades but wouldn't be amongst the top 20-30 students.

I can't forget this incident. The falling of that Star was a rare sight, but why should it leave an impression in my mind? Because certain significant changes took place in my life soon after that incident.

The first change was that after the 8th class, we had to select our Stream of Studies. I knew I would select Science. I wanted to become a Research Scientist or an Engineer, because my maternal uncle, who influenced my life, was an Engineer. So, when I was taken in 9th Class, I was to be selected for the Science section, but I was rejected as my 8th class results were not up to the mark. I couldn't get into the Science section. For a week or so, I attended Arts class, and then I got a message that one seat had been vacated, and I was the next one who could be allocated that seat in the science class. The teachers of the school advised me not to select science because that career was not suitable for boys who were average or poor in studies. That career was very competitive; only top-class boys could make their career in engineering. But against all their advice, I opted for it and became a science student.

Science and mathematics teachers used to make fun of me because they thought I was not a suitable candidate for their subjects. But the strange thing was, within a few days, my mathematics teacher brought out a problem that he had not solved for many years. I solved that problem for him. He was shocked and looked at me with suspicion. I succeeded in even solving the complex problem that he selected for me. He was so impressed by me that within a few months I became his best boy. I was treated like a star and became very popular amongst teachers in the 9th class. Although it is a different story, in 9th class in the final exams, the boy who stood first got 600 marks, I got 599 and I stood second. That was strange enough for everybody that I could reach such heights.

The third strange incident happened when I appeared for Higher Secondary 11th class exams. I never studied hard. I used to feel that I knew everything. I would flip over the pages and feel like I had read the whole book. I do not know how. Or I would just glance at the book and feel I knew every subject well. Most of my time was spent playing instead of studying. We were very poor, and I was physically weak because my diet was poor. But when I appeared for Higher secondary, I knew I had done well. Our neighbor who was working at the University asked for my roll number and said he could bring my result four days before. I gave him my number 2203, and he brought the result the next day and told me I passed in the 2nd Division. My Mother was pleased. She was afraid that if I got First Division or Distinction, I might be selected and given a Scholarship for Higher studies which she didn't want.

She said, "Look, Ram, We are very poor. We are not able to maintain our family. You are the eldest son of our family. After passing Higher Secondary, you must search for a job and work to support the family."

Even though I would get a Scholarship, the idea of me studying further was not appealing to her. She said that she was thrilled that I got the Second Division. I was very disappointed, and I was in tears.

I said, *"Ma, something is not right. I have to be on top. I cannot be in the 2nd division. If I were in the second division, none in the class would get first division, which I am sure of. Something is wrong. This cannot be my result".*

I was so confident that I approached the neighbor and asked him to re-check my roll-no. The next day, he again brought the result and said, "*You have got second division.*"

Everybody accepted that I had got second division. But I waited for the final results. When the final results came in the morning, on the due date, in the Newspaper, I found myself on the Merit list, not only First Class but with Distinction, and I was 10th in the University. Imagine my confidence; I got admission without any difficulty with Scholarships in Engineering. The Scholarship given to me was Rs 100/- per month, which was a considerable amount at that time, because my father used to earn only Rs 180/- per month, after 40 years of service in Telephone exchange. My scholarship took care of my studies and partly supported the family's expenses.

Early Life

I was a brilliant student in my college days and acknowledged as a mathematics wizard. My parents could not afford to pay for my education but fortunately for me, I earned a scholarship throughout my study period. I passed my Engineering degree in 1959 from Delhi University and applied for a job in few companies. I applied for a Government job at UPSC and Tatas, and I was selected by both organizations. I accepted the job at Tata. In 1963, I got married to Savitri. After Seven years of working in Tata, I left Delhi to go to Bombay with my family, wife & three kids. My youngest daughter (fourth child) was born in Bombay.

I found a job with a Sindhi Seth in Mumbai, but due to my boss's health issue and his subsequent death, I lost the job suddenly and was left in a lurch. In those days, it was not easy to get a job. In panic and under tension, I joined a firm by promising to create a machine that was not available in India to produce PVC (Polyvinyl chloride) slippers for him. Importing a Machine from Germany at Rupees 60 to 70 lakhs was not feasible. I was confident that I could design and build such a machine locally. Seeing my confidence and the details I worked out, I got lucrative payment terms from him with an excellent salary, a beautiful bungalow and a car with a driver.

All I did was convert an old, cheap machine to make it suitable for production at a minimum cost of Rs 2.5 lakhs. It took almost a year to complete the task.

After starting production, within a year, the life of my boss changed. He was the sole distributor of PVC slippers, and he flourished.

As per the agreement, I was supposed to be a partner in the future profits of this company. But greed overtook him and he did not fulfill his promise. I was young and a novice. My agreement with him was not perfect and taking advantage of the same; he denied my remuneration and benefits. I left him in anger.

His competitor from Mumbai, Marwari fellow, was observing me and immediately offered me Rs. 50,000 as a down payment to make the same type of machine for him. I had left the earlier company after deciding to start my own business. After preparing the drawing of that machine and signing an agreement on stamp paper I received the down payment. I bought a factory in Pune by paying only the 1st installment of Rs.8,000. As per the terms, I did not have to pay anything for another ten years and after ten years, I had to pay Rs. 8,000 per year for 20 years.

I also bought a House of my own on installments of Rs. 1,000 only and a car for Rs.10,000 because I was accustomed to cars in Bombay. Furthermore, I took an apartment on rent in Bombay after paying a deposit of Rs. 10,000. The rent was Rs 350 per month.

I started a Consultation business on my own, consulting fees starting from Rs.50,000 and upwards. The factory where I invested Rs. 8,000 at that time is now giving me an income of 5 lakhs as rent per month. Can you imagine the value of Rs. 8,000 at that time?

Unfortunately, the design of the machine I made for my previous boss was copied and available in the market. I had to look for other alternatives. I had gained enough confidence since my machine had clicked. It created a huge positive change in the market. I went on to invent many more items, almost 30 to 40 of which were not available in India then, earning huge returns particularly from 3 to 4 inventions.

My first invention was the *Automatic Electronic Solid State panel,* for the type of machines I had manufactured in Hyderabad & Mumbai. Formerly those machines were fitted with an electric panel of 6 feet height with many electrical appliances attached. Instead, I created a replacement for that in a small electronic panel that could be carried in hand. It was only 4″ to 6″ in height. The panel cost was also reduced from an initial cost of Rs 35,000 per month to Rs 700. I sold the panel for Rs. 3,000 to one of the companies manufacturing these automatic machines. They were eager to get it as it reduced their cost considerably from Rs. 35,000 to Rs. 3,000.

Previously if the panel had any problem, they had to locate & repair it, but in this case, they would dispose of the capsule to replace it with a new one. I earned a lot of money on this invention as well.

Next, I made *solid State Annunciators* for Otis elevators. Otis was an International company. They approached me to make the above part. They mentioned having a severe problem with the relays which operated in lifts. The relays used to get damaged due to the vibration when the lifts were used. They had to repair or replace them. The company's reputation was at stake.

I designed the immovable solid case annunciators, the same size as the relay, and could easily replace the damaged piece. It was a huge success. They must have bought a few lakhs of those pieces from me. It cost me Rs 4 only whereas I sold it to them for about 35 to 40 rupees. I again made a lot from this invention. I also developed *Electronic Timers.*

This is how I made good money. Later, I bought a few machines for my own company and took up jobs for factories to produce parts or machines unavailable in India. Twenty years of my life, from 1970 to 1990, were spent inventing, producing and distributing. Finally I had made enough money to pay my taxes and retire.

I can say it was the Grace of Narayana, that kept guiding me all through my life. Business or personal life whatever I have been through was all due to His grace.

I have gone through some miracles in my life in the past. I remember them and now, I will reveal them and describe the miracles in detail one by one.

The 1st miracle happened in 1970. I was 33 yrs old at that time. I decided to go on a holiday with my wife, one son, three daughters and my 65 yr old father. We decided to take a road trip. We all started on a journey in a small standard Herald car from Hyderabad towards south to Kanyakumari. The body of the car was very thin. We comfortably settled in the car and drove from Hyderabad to Madras in Tamilnadu. Every day we covered approximately 400 km. We rented a place at night and moved ahead in the morning. It was enjoyable traveling this way, eating food at various places and cities, seeing a little bit of the city around us and moving on ahead.

Visit To Tirupati

On our way to Madras (renamed as Chennai), a friend suggested we visit the Tirupati temple on a mountain top. I did not believe in temples, prayers, or God, as I felt people projected this out of their minds due to fear. It is better to live a life of creativity, intelligence and wisdom. He further mentioned that since it was situated on a mountain the weather was excellent and as it was a small town it was easy to find accommodation at a reasonable price. The surroundings are alive and joyful. *You will enjoy your stay there even if you do not see the temple.*

I liked the suggestion and we visited Tirupati. We got suitable accommodation and our three days stay was comfortable. We observed an extraordinary sight there. There would be long queues of devotees throughout the day and the night for 24 hours chanting *Govinda, Govinda, Venkateshwara Govinda.* They would enter the temple with flowers and fruits as offerings to the Lord, prayed and asked for whatever was their need and came out satisfied.

Moving around in the city were thousands of devotees, both ladies and gents going towards a hall where hundreds of barbers were busy cutting off beautiful long tresses of ladies. Both men and women would get their heads shaved off. An unending sea of devotees entered one after the other. It was a sight to behold.

I was surprised to see people's faith and devotion to the point where I started to doubt my method of meditation. I felt that maybe there was a Power. God may not be there in person, but there is some power in the stone statue of Tirupati. So many people cannot be wrong. With this thought, I did an action very unlike me. I wanted to experience what these devotees were experiencing. So I too bought fruits and flowers, prayed and got my head shaved off. I prayed and asked for a boon that seemed almost impossible to me then. I would find out if my prayer was answered. The priest gave us big huge ladoos as prasad. There were a lot of monkeys around and one of them snatched one ladoo from us. It was amusing.

After praying, we moved further down south towards Kanyakumari. In a few days, I forgot about my prayer to Lord Tirupati. I forgot I had asked for the impossible as I did not expect my prayer to be fulfilled.

On my way back from Kanyakumari, I visited Bangalore. Distance between Bangalore and Hyderabad was approximately 500 km. On our way to Hyderabad, I completed about 200 km in a day and booked a hotel room for the night. The next day we started driving. A bullock cart in front of us blocked our way and slowed us down considerably. While trying to overtake the bullock-cart, we had a major accident. My car slipped and overturned several times until finally, it landed upside down on its roof. The chassis was bent & the glass around the car had shattered completely. All four doors were damaged.

My youngest daughter had flown out of the car window and had landed on the road about 60 feet away. The rest of us were still in the car. I quickly appraised the situation around me. With no visible signs of a wound to ourselves, I carefully slipped out of the car and picked up my daughter from the road. My wife was in shock and had a short-term (about 2hrs) memory loss. The police quickly came to our assistance. They helped us to move to a nearby hospital. Although none of us were physically hurt, the seriousness of the accident caused a mental disturbance. We stayed in the hospital for two days. The doctors and nurses were very helpful.

Again, in the area where the hospital was, there were a lot of monkeys around us. They amused us with their funny pranks, a sight to behold. We enjoyed their company.

I immediately called the company where I worked to send us a new car and to tow away the badly damaged one. Since the car was beyond recognition, it was a total write-off. My boss handled the formalities for the car and sent us a new one.

I realized Lord Tirupati had protected us. It was a miraculous escape from death. All of us were unhurt and safe despite the severe accident. The boon I had prayed for was to have my own Company. I was always working under someone all the way. My boss used to pay me very well in addition to the perks such as a bungalow and a car to move around. The facilities were good in the company and we were pretty comfortable. If I decided to become my boss, I would have to leave this job and in turn all the perks.

Without any money in my bank account, the desire to start my own business and be able to earn enough to get some of those luxuries immediately, looked almost impossible. Hence my prayer to Lord Tirupati seemed unrealistic and unachievable to me.

However, look at the turn of events. The accident created some tensions between my boss and I. My ego did not permit me to continue working with him and I left the job. Here I was with nothing in hand. With little savings, I started a small manufacturing unit.. Unexpectedly an offer of help came from a businessman Mr. Manu from Bombay. He was interested in my inventions as he had seen me perform well at my earlier job. He gave me a down payment of Rs 50,000, so I could create the items for him. The down payment was a considerable amount at that time & it was not only enough to start my own business, but I could even rent a flat in Bombay and buy a car as well. I finally became the boss of my own company with the blessings of Lord Tirupati.

Ram, during his younger days, as proprietor of his co.Pesh Enterprises

Ram, with a shaved head, after a visit from Tirupati, during Gitas engagement

Grandsons Ish & Raj

Swami Brahmchariji

GuruPrasad Aminji with his wife Sujayaji

Poonam Renu Sunil Gitu Ram & Savitri Peswani

After this one incident, I still had doubts. My mind refused to accept that there was some higher power or God. So later on, I went to Tirupati three to four times and tested the power of Tirupati by asking for some minor boons, which later on, got granted. After ten years or so, I was pretty sure there may or may not be God, but there are some higher powers that we cannot see through our senses but they do influence our lives. I thought when I was free of responsibilities. I would devote my time to researching the topic further and find if we can contact higher powers or achieve high powers. I was convinced Lord Tirupati had some higher powers. When I went to Tirupati, I said to God, *"This is my last boon, do me a favor and make me like you, rather than come to you again and again and ask you for something."*

On my visit to Tirupati, I asked Lord Tirupati for a boon. *I wanted to be like Him.* With His blessings and my dedication, I believed that would happen.

In my entire life, I have shaved my head thrice during my visits to Tirupati. I remember once I came back home with a shaved head and reduced weight at age 50. My family members did not recognize me at Pune railway station. I had a good laugh when I had to introduce myself to them.

Two more incidents in my younger age changed my attitude towards Meditation. The first was about my maternal uncle. He used to meditate a lot, and he also had a Guru. He acquired some power and was very well respected because of this power. He was an engineer in a military service workshop. After acquiring powers, he fell in love with a Muslim girl. This love was so intense that he fought with both Hindu and Muslim communities, including his wife, children, and office staff. He had to convert to Islam to marry that girl. He had two children from her and eight from his first wife. This situation was a daily torment for his first wife, who died cursing the situation she faced with no respite.

It created an impression in my mind that meditation alone is not adequate and can be dangerous. One should have control over one's basic nature.

Another incident was my habit of taking one month's leave from my job and wandering around India by car.

But at later stages, I used to leave my family with the children's maternal grandfather in Delhi and go alone to the Himalayas. I used to visit Gangotri, Yamunotri, Kedarnath, Badrinath, Chamba, etc., where I came in contact with many wandering saints. Many of these Saints were aimless and were lost souls. They were neither fit for family life nor spirituality.

Spirituality is not a simple phenomenon, it requires one to leave everything and enter uncharted waters. It is the biggest gamble of life and nobody can guarantee awakening or enlightenment.

So before the age of 50, I had made three decisions. The first was to persistently search for higher powers like that exist in Tirupati and other places and experience them. The Second was to avoid the meditation process practiced by my maternal uncle which harmed the society. Third was to avoid the path followed by the saints in the Himalayas who, according to me, were wasting their time and were highly frustrated.

Chapter 3

"Train your eyes and ears; train your nose and tongue. The senses are good friends when they are trained. Train your body in deeds, train your tongue in words, train your mind in thoughts. This training will take you beyond sorrow."

~ Buddha[9]

Inward Journey

I was never satisfied or happy and content in spite of all my wealth. There was a storm raging within me. There were many questions for which I had no answers. I wanted to know,

Why had I come into this Universe?

What is the purpose of my existence?

What is the meaning of this life?

I had a good life and a family with four children, and I was very content with the way they were all evolving, yet I needed answers to my questions. So as per my plan, after earning enough and giving a secure life to

---

9 Courtesy: https://nenp.facebook.com/ValueBuddhaDhamma/photos/train-your-eyes-and-ears-train-your-nose-and-tongue-the-senses-are-good-friends-/1835006316672001/

my family, I started thinking about doing something about my questions.

After retirement from my service and business, I spent many hours daily for 36 years of my life in austere meditation. As a result, I understood that some 2560 years back, Gautam Buddha came to the Earth, and he was taken to be God. According to Him, meditation was the way to achieve God. One had to go within to get answers and gain wisdom.

Then came Jesus Christ 2000 and odd years ago. He is believed to be the Son of God and preached compassion, love and brotherhood. He absorbed the misery and negativity of others and freed them from pain and suffering. Many people became his disciples and devotees.

Prophet Muhammad came in 570 CE[10]. They called him the Prophet, a realized soul. He stayed in a cave to achieve Self-realization. Prophet Muhammad said that when he was in the cave, a Saint called Gabriel used to visit him. He summarized his knowledge to the point that there is a God, yet there is no God, that it has no form, no shape, and is empty in this vast Universe. Mohammad, the Prophet, was told by Saint Gabriel to learn to take energy and take actions as per his understanding. He had the energy to soak the negativities. Mohammad followed the teachings of the

---

10 Muhammad, the Messenger of God."inscribed on the gates of the Prophet's Mosque in Medina born. 570 CE (Courtesy : https://en.wikipedia.org/wiki/Muhammad)

Void, and many people became his disciples and took advantage of His teachings.

From the teachings of all the three saints, I learned that when we meditate and go within, we connect with the Higher Source and some energies, powers, and beings enter within to guide us. They help us with the life ahead and show our purpose.

Quenching My Thirst Finally At God's Fountain

I prepared myself to go into deep meditation 30 years ago at age 55 and went to Igatpuri, where Gautam Buddha's Vipassana Meditation courses are held. To my great surprise some spiritual voice started talking to me on the first night itself. I can never forget that day; 30th June 1992, an unforgettable event. This great entity has been holding my hand and guiding me ever since.

Let's start from the time my Spiritual Journey started. I was 50 yrs old. My son, Sunil, had gone to America to study, and my eldest daughter was in her final year of Engineering and was engaged. My factories ran smoothly, good income flowed, and my bank balance was good. But I was not keeping well. There was a painful ulcer in my throat for some time. It was not healing, and I didn't particularly appreciate going to doctors, fearing that they might say it was Cancer.

I also had a migraine that would prolong for a week and make my life painful. Besides, I had other health problems and was unhappy with them. I thought that maybe I had made some mistakes in life that induced these health problems.

So I decided that after completing my family responsibilities and marrying off my two younger daughters in the next five years, I would search for this knowledge. When I would reach the age of 55, I would search for God or Higher Powers and their mode of existence by selecting an appropriate method. I knew it was a difficult path. I had seen many failures. So if I was to choose this option after thorough consideration, there was no way I could return. So I would hand over all my properties and factories to my children by the age of 55 so that I could never choose the option of returning. This way I would close all my options of returning to worldly life and succeed in finding a suitable meditation method.

In the next 5 years, I did what I planned. I joined the course at Igatpuri, Vipassana meditation, on 30th June 1992. My son was back from America, and I decided to hand over the responsibilities of the factories to him. I informed my family that I was going to the jungle.

When my family realised my seriousness and determination in my pursuit of spirituality, they requested me not to leave the house. They assured me that I would not be disturbed in a closed room of the house and would only meet me to serve food. After much discussion, I decided that after completing the course at Igatpuri I would stay home and continue meditation behind closed doors.

I will tell you about my first-night stay incident at Igatpuri, on 30th June 1992. This was a big miracle. After that incident, my life changed. The very first night when I slept, I kept pondering whether there was anything like KARMAS. If Karmas existed, we must be accumulating Karmas every now and then. *Who keeps records of our Karmas?*

I must have taken many births and lived many lives. Accumulated number of Karmas from all these lives that could be as vast as the ocean.

Where is the record kept? In my body or Soul?

What must I do to reap the results of my Karmas?

These questions perplexed me a lot. That night, I dreamt that a Higher Power came into my contact. Interestingly after the night's dream, I stopped having migraines and my ulcer gradually disappeared.

Thinking of it now, I feel it must be Tirupati's Narayana, a high-power source. I had asked Him to make me like Him or like Buddha during my previous visit to Tirupati temple, or it might be Gautam Buddha who relieved me of my illness. I did not know.

That power has kept guiding and talking to me every day of my life till now, since 30th June 1992. I have got answers to most of my questions.

That night, I had asked, '*How do I read the record of my Karmas?*' He gave me a special vision in which I could perceive my whole body. My body looked like the Universe with stars, Milky way, Galaxy, and Sky.

My inner voice explained that the cosmic factor which is present in our body keeps track of our Karmas. To understand this process, we can take the example of a tiny microchip of a computer, where massive data is written and stored which could be retrieved when desired. In the same way in my body, cosmic electrons are present, which keep track of effects of the astral body, extract energies from that body, and keep the Karmas updated all the time.

I had asked, *" What should I do to avoid going through the Karmas?"*

He had replied "You have one type of energy which is in the form of **Awareness**. Close your eyes and watch your internal energy for which you can perceive different sensations. *See the **Sensations** through that Awareness; then, those Karmas will dissolve. From the Universe you have created these in your body. Select each Sensation and dissolve it with your closed eyes. It has caused so much suffering. Empty it by selecting each Karma. That will be the meditation technique for You from now on"*

I was asked by my internal Guide/ Guru to do meditation with internal awareness & dissolve all Karmas. The guide had said "The Karmas will start dissolving as you keep observing your Sensations. This will be your meditation."

I liked this method as I found it easy. After completing my ten day Vipassana course, I came home determined to continue meditating. I sat behind closed doors for 12 hours at a stretch daily for two years and meditated by observing my sensations. I saw my Karmas dissolve.

This form of meditation became an exciting game for me. I never got bored and sat for long hours meditating. It became my hobby and whether awake or asleep, I was meditating nonstop. After doing this form of meditation for a couple of years, another serious miracle happened in my life.

One day while in meditation, I observed a huge entity in my body. It looked dangerous. I thought I could break this entity with awareness and free myself of it.

Yes I saw a formation in my body and I have called it an entity. It was always a pattern of energies with different colors. And some of them looked aggressive in color and design.

This pattern as huge as my body covering me from head to feet. I would call it a *Demon*. Or if the pattern is over my head who could read my mind, I would refer to it as *Ghost*.

If I did not break it, this entity would grow further and make my health suffer. This looked serious. *Obtaining enough courage from my inner Guru, I sat down with the gift of awareness.*

The next day my son Sunil came running in panic to me and informed me that my small factory, Ranco

Enterprises, had caught fire and we had suffered heavy losses.

I knew I had taken up the arduous task of clearing negative entities within, which was directly impacting my outside world. But I didn't feel confident enough to speak about it with my son. I kept quiet and continued, meditating to dissolve the entity with further zeal and enthusiasm, thereby ignoring the fire in my factory and losses in crores of Rupees.

I finally managed to dissolve this entity. But no sooner had I achieved success, I saw an even larger entity, 3 to 4 times in size of the earlier one and more dangerous. A thought crossed my mind. Was this entity connected to my second factory, Palonji Pvt Ltd., which was much bigger? Ranco Enterprises had already been burnt. If I attacked this new entity with my awareness, would Palonji Pvt Ltd. also be destroyed? I was in a dilemma. Should I stop meditating?

Not to meditate meant I would not be able to dissolve my Karmas. An Inner Voice told me, *Do not be worried, my son. These entities are related to your negative Karma, ultimately making you suffer. By clearing these entities, you will free yourself from Karmas and benefit from it.* In this way, I was encouraged and with that boost, I sat down to meditate. Everything looked normal with no adverse effects around me for many days until one day Sunil gave me the terrible news. Palonji Pvt. Ltd. had also caught fire and we suffered heavy losses.

This time I was wiser. I laughed and told him, "I know our factory has caught fire, but I cannot come there to help you put out the fire. I will rectify the situation internally. You go and do what you can to salvage the factory in whatever way you can."

Fortunately, there was no loss of life. We had a massive financial setback, but I was more prepared this time.

After both the factories were burnt and destroyed we had further problems. Since Sunil had studied abroad, he did not have field experience handling laborers. They went on strike because of which Sunil had trouble in producing goods. My whole world came tumbling down, in terms of the factories, production, stock of goods, everything.

The great news was that Sunil could rent out those factories within a few months for rupees 5 Lakhs, which was my original income from the regular operations of the two factories.

Now, look at the miraculous turnaround. Earlier we were getting five lakhs after slogging a lot, but now we were getting the same amount from the rent without any effort .

Sunil became free. Anyway he did not have any interest in those factories . With regular income coming in, he showed the courage to fulfill his desire. With his effort, he entered the IT Industry as he had studied abroad and obtained the degree in the same. Very soon, he flourished and prospered. It was the right time for him. His future was made.

With the above incidents in life, I had a great learning experience. All these incidents took place not by accident but these were all planned by God. I had to undergo these hardships and grow stronger to face further challenges to fulfil the task assigned to me. My will power and determination further increased and I continued with my meditation process undeterred.

My Outside world was Interconnected with my Inner world. My continued meditation, sitting in my room behind closed doors, drastically changed my outside world. I have understood that initial hurdles and difficulties pave the way for success in attaining our objectives.

This learning further increased my enthusiasm to meditate as I felt guided to **clear & cleanse** my astral body of all entities/ Karmas to become one with the Higher Power.

This is just a thought, but I still have to tell you what happened further.

I felt fortunate to have met my Inner Guru on 30th June and be given the experiential knowledge of the connection between the internal & external world. I realized that my wife, kids, house, and relatives were all linked with my Karma in the external world. I could take care of them, too, internally.

In all this drama, my wife has been a strong pillar of the family. We are forever indebted to her. She is a very pious and chaste soul and has been quite encouraging and supportive in all our ventures. I think that enduring committed love between us and raising children in a loving environment are the Noblest acts anyone can aspire for. She has dedicated her whole life to keeping us happy and catering to all our family needs. She has raised children well, is a strict disciplinarian, and prays to Hindu Gods and Guru Nanak Ji. She feeds poor people on Gurupurab days and holds Satnarayan pujas. When our Ventures started, she showed gratitude to God by holding a small puja. Children have learned a lot and are brilliant in whatever they do. God has been kind to us.

I continued with my meditation inside my body through the sensations. On 30th June 1992, the first night in Vipassana Centre at Igatpuri, I had either a dream or a vision because I saw Stars in my astral body after I went to sleep. So you can call that a dream or vision. *Later, I was told that when these micro cosmic particles (which I call Stars) which were formed due to past Karmas change with awareness due to meditation, they cause sensations, and I have to observe them, so all my subsequent meditations were on sensation.*

This Voice that started speaking to me and guiding, now I say, his name was Narayana, was very powerful. When I meditated in Igatpuri Ashram in the Vipassana course, Loudspeaker would blare out some instructions every 10-15 minutes. This Inner Voice said that you have only to *observe your sensation* and not bother about the method they preach.

That ten-day course of Igatpuri also advised watching *Sensations,* but they asked people to watch *Sensations* on the body's surface. They specifically instructed that one should not go inside the body, but they also told us that for the first three days not to watch these Sensations but concentrate and increase the Awareness. After three days, when the concentration had increased, and Awareness strength had increased, they asked us to watch only the Sensation. On the 9th day, they asked us to change the meditation method and reverse it, and they called it ***Metta meditation.***[11]

While my Inside Voice said, "Do not bother about these instructions, watch these Sensations deep inside your body, which are the formation of Stars, and there your Sensation will make you feel their form".

---

11 Metta Meditation (Courtesy : https://oneminddharma.com/what-is-metta/ (ref Appendix pg xxvii)

So, I was surprised that loudspeakers were blaring every 15 minutes giving us instructions, and yet I'd only be able to follow the instructions of my Inside Voice which was so powerful .

My migraine headache disappeared on the first night, on 30th June 1992, and it never returned in my life. The instructions at Igatpuri were also that you leave the ten-day course, after doing Metta meditation. On the tenth day when you go home, do not meditate for more than one or two hours every day, and every one or two hours when you want to stop the meditation, the last ten minutes should be devoted to Metta meditation.

Metta meditation is the reverse of the Meditation of Emptiness[12], i.e., Awareness whereby Sensations fade

12 What is Metta? – Metta Practice, Meditations, and Explanation.(ref Appendix pg xxvii)

away. It is refilling the Sensations but of *positiveness, of love* towards the whole of universe. The reason given was that at the end of the 10 day course, if you do not do Metta meditation, *then your surface body will be empty of all Sensations; and some negative Spirits, like Bhoot, Pret or some dangerous Spirits, may occupy that area and create havoc in your life.* It is extremely important, according to their curriculum, that Metta should be practiced at the end of the course. It is also told that, at home, after completing one or two hours of meditation, Metta should be performed .

In contrast my Inner Voice told me not to bother about *Bhoot, Pret* or negativity, just continue meditating without bothering about the two hours limitation on meditation. You continue to dissolve your Karmas, go deep inside, and do not remain on the surface. I followed this process for the next two years in my house. In between I used to visit Igatpuri for a ten-day refresher course . Once every 3-4 months, I used to get into the environment and listen to their talks.

Many things about Gautam Buddha were told to me at Igatpuri including that Gautam Buddha had devised this meditation method. The most important thing they told me that impressed my mind was that **Buddha wanted the whole community and this world to be free from old age and mental and physical sufferings, death, and fear of those sufferings.** This was the

---

(Courtesy : https://oneminddharma.com/what-is-metta/)

ultimate objective that Gautam Buddha had given to his meditating disciples.

The Transition

I believe there are some very powerful saints in India because they have a considerable following and powers backing them. They might know of the wisdom I was receiving internally. Accordingly, I planned a trip with a friend to meet a saint from Chamba in 1993. Before becoming a saint, he was called Rajinder. I used to call him Swamiji, Swami Brahmchariji.

We planned to visit several Ashrams across India in my car and started our journey from Pune. During the past few years, Swamiji had been elevated to a higher level of saints and was given an ashram at Chamba, which he managed. Swamiji was acquainted with different saints across India who had considerable following.

At that time, I had a Qualis car. I removed the back seat from the car and made arrangements for sleeping with an attached WC for emergency use. It was a month long trip. We started from Pune and drove through Rajasthan, Punjab, and Himachal Pradesh up to Ladakh. On the way back, we drove from Delhi down to Banaras, Calcutta and back to Pune. It was a long trip. We visited several Ashrams and met many saints whom Swamiji knew. Swamiji used to introduce me to them. However, I (Ram Peswani) was not in saintly clothes; I meditated a lot and had received enormous knowledge but I wanted to enhance it with the help of their experience and clear some of my doubts.

The Swamis in the ashrams listened aptly to me. They all gave me a lot of respect. *They humbled me although they were powerful saints with a huge following; they gave me a good place to stay* and tried to make my stay as comfortable as possible. After hearing me out, their only comment was that there is something we do not understand about you, but we think you are on the right path.

That statement did not help me at all. It made me think further. Either my knowledge was incorrect, or if it was correct, then it was different from their knowledge.

A Ray of Hope

One beautiful morning during my relentless search, I came across an *article* on the internet, which perfectly matched my thoughts and learnings.

I was excited beyond limits. My eternal search of 20 years had borne fruit in the form of information on the Net. I dug deeper into it and found out that the chapter was a part of the *Lotus Sutra,* which was spoken by Gautam Buddha 2560 years ago in Pali language. It was later translated into Sanskrit, Chinese, and many other languages.

English translation of Lotus Sutra by Burton Watson[13] was also available in India. I had to get a copy of that book, come what may. My search for that book began. Luckily someone knew about it and mentioned it was available in Dharamshala near Chamba, where the Dalai Lama had his Ashram.

I could not wait any longer and visited Dharamshala as soon as possible. I bought a few copies of The Lotus Sutra and have read it several times since then.

As explained earlier I had been following the instructions given by my inner voice but at times I kept wondering if I am on the right path on my meditation process. Instructions from Igatpuri and different viewpoints expressed in many forums on websites and also my own past experiences with Gurus in the Himalayas and other places had created uncertainties in my mind. However after going through Lotus Sutra, all my questions were adequately answered. Things became crystal clear on the right path of salvation. This book confirmed that the knowledge I received was indeed priceless. The Lotus Sutra serves me as a Bible now.

---

13 Lotus Sutra translated by Burton Watson.

(Courtesy :

https://ia802902.us.archive.org/13/items/lotussutraburtonwatson_202003_473_o/Lotus%20Sutra%20Burton%20Watson.pdf)

Later on, I will give you more information about Lotus Sutra. It has been my Guru and Guide and will stay with me forever.

I remember one more incident when I was caught in a dilemma in 1995. After my son's factory was engulfed in a huge fire, it was still working to some extent, but post fire, there was extreme labor trouble. Because of this situation and the financial losses they were going through and probably because of some family issues that Gitu, my daughter, was going through, Gitu, Sunil and my wife came to me and requested me to stop the meditation. They assumed that the disasters and difficulties faced by the family were due to my meditation. They strongly felt that I must be following some wrong practices in meditation.

The representation was solid from their side, and I got worried. When I meditated again, the strong voice of Narayana told me not to worry. This obstacle would also pass away. My family suggested that *"if you do not want to stop meditation, let us all proceed to Igatpuri- Nasik, meet your Guru there, who taught you Vipassana, and consult him. If you are making some mistakes, you will also come to know so that you can change your meditation method. If you still feel that you are on the right path of meditation, we won't bother you, and you can continue with your way of meditation"*. I knew that Nasik teachers would condemn my meditation because I was neither doing Metta nor was I following their rule of limiting my meditation duration to an hour or two in a day. But as I had assurance within me from the Voice of Narayana, *"Don't bother, nothing will happen,"* it made me bold enough to agree with my family.

So we drove in our car from Pune to Igatpuri, Nasik. We met the teacher there. When the teacher heard what I was doing, he was shocked. He was totally against the way I did my meditation. He said such a meditation process was precarious, and my family would face severe disturbance. He told my family that I was following the wrong process of meditation. He continued, *"He is not following our system, and there has been a bad case in our group with a man who disobeyed the rules and meditated without Metta Bhavna. He became mad, and his business was ruined. His whole family was destroyed, and he wanders like a madman with torn clothes in the jungle. Whatever your father is doing will lead you to destruction".* He condemned my meditation and stressed it would lead to disastrous consequences.

My family was calm even after getting such an adverse reaction from the teacher on my method of Meditation. It was my biggest surprise when such a strong statement was made to my family, but they were unaffected. We returned to Pune, and they never said anything further. They kept up with their promise. I continued to do my meditation. This Vipassana incident happened around the year 1995.

Chapter 4

"When the mind is silent like a lake the lotus blossoms." [14]

Wish- Granting Jewel

In deep meditation, I was guided to go past the obstacles and crucial points in my life, which were, on their own, unique. I used to sit for hours in meditation. I tried making notes of the learnings/ experiences, which ran into a few hundred pages. The knowledge was unique and mentioned in Ved Shastras, holy talks, etc. Gautam Buddha called it THE LOTUS SUTRA. The Buddhists worship it, but very few understand it fully.

After a lot of research, I located the Lotus Sutra but even after reading it multiple times could not understand much of it. I spoke to many Buddhist followers and disciples from all over the world on forums and on the internet, but no one could give me a satisfactory explanation of the real knowledge in it. So I again sat down to meditate and asked the Guru within. After delving deep into each point for the last 30 years, I have understood it, and I am convinced that the UNIVERSE is Empty and it is all Maya all over.

---

14 Courtesy: https://www.goodreads.com/quotes/8843588-when-the-mind-is-silent-like-a-lake-the-lotus

Gautam Buddha too reiterated that the governing force of it all, is **Emptiness.**

I had to maintain a state where the Universe exists and also that it does not exist. I exist and that I do not exist. When you come to that State where you are NOTHING, everything becomes clear. Your awareness expands and you can see your body within with much clarity.

I was told to walk on this path with understanding. It is possible to walk on this path only if you have this body. Nothing is under your control, but your body is yours. If you have health problems, physical or mental, it is because you have done something which has not been right. It is up to you to rectify that problem, which you can do by going within your body to understand its intricacy. Your health improves when you focus on the painful part of your body with awareness.

With the tool of awareness, we can make this creation a beautiful place to live. Through awareness in your body, you balance the mistakes and rise above your weakness, thereby rectifying your karma and getting yourself in a state of total peace.

Opening the Lock To Lotus Sutra

After about two years of joining Vipassana meditation i.e. 1994, the secret of the Universe was revealed to me. I was made aware that I am not a separate entity. I am connected to everyone. I am connected to my family, relatives, and the whole world. In the state of emptiness, minute cells/atoms connect to others and that's how it becomes possible to help others. I understood that we could make the whole creation beautiful when we free ourselves from negativities. I found this revelation strange and experimented on it, which I will discuss in detail in the later chapters.

I experimented under the guidance of my Inner Guru. As I continued to evolve from within, a question arose. I did understand that the mistakes I made could be rectified with Awareness, *but what about certain beliefs, thought patterns and ideas residing in me through eons of time from sources beyond my reach? How was I to remove them?*

As I went within, the pearls of Wisdom started flowing. My Inner Guru advised me to study and understand the Lotus Sutra in depth. **When you become one with the Lotus Sutra, it starts talking to you. Gautam Buddha got this knowledge, and he shared it with us.**

Many years ago, when the Stars and Moon did not exist, the Universe was in formation. Universes were created and lost in different forms. Different species were born and destroyed. If you study the Lotus Sutra, you can get this knowledge. Lotus Sutra has millions of years of knowledge in it.

To continue further with my story, I used to keep a chart of the level of intensity of these negative body Sensations (micro vibrations in small areas of the body. eg. Eye twitching is one of the commonly known vibrations caused by some medical condition) in my body on a piece of paper, and as time passed, these decreased considerably, and after two years, I felt there were hardly any abnormalities left in my body.

I was pleased that there was no disease and the pain due to the ulcer had subsided; though it was deep inside my body, I was not feeling it. I felt very light and had no pain or discomfort in my body. I thought I had achieved such a significant positive change in my body due to the result of the high level of my meditation process.

On the other hand positive physical sensations were on the rise, and everything was felt at higher level frequency and intensity. I would experience the deep silence as well as I could hear very faint vibrations. I could hear the horns of vehicles from far away. I heard numerous birds chirping, which I had never experienced before. I was very calm, extremely peaceful and felt I was no longer the same old person. But nobody in my surroundings felt any change in me. I was surprised and wondered why they did not feel it.

Inner Voice Guidance

I had done great things during those two years, meditating for 12 hours a day. I had completely dissolved my negative Karmas, yet nobody saw the difference in me. So I asked my Inner Voice, by then I knew he was Narayana, *"I feel a great change in me but others around me have no clue about it. At Igatpuri, they told me that Gautam Buddha's power that impacted the whole Universe, was felt strongly by all people around him. But, I cannot make anybody feel anything about my achievement". Unless people realise my achievement and accept me as the enlightened one, I will not be able to spread the message of Lotus Sutra. That is the reason I had asked my inner voice to make me like Buddha in the past.*

I expressed my desire to become like Buddha once again. The Voice told me to forget being Gautam Buddha, which was an impossible task and beyond my capacity. Buddha had meditated a thousand fold more than what I did which was about 12 hrs a day for two years. I felt very strange. After one or two days, I still felt restless.

I asked Him again, *"No, I am not happy. I want to become Buddha. Show me the way".*

The Voice said, *"Forget about it. It's too difficult. You can't do it, and I won't be able to guide you because there is a lot of difference between Buddha and you."*

A couple of days later, I said, "*Look, I thought it over carefully.*" The Emptiness that had come into me when I could not see Stars in my body made me feel that I have no Ego; I am Nothing. I am absolutely Nothing.

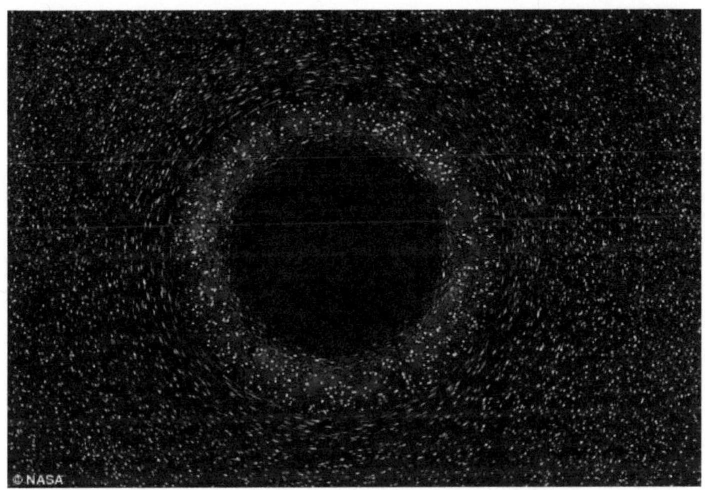

In order for someone to experience true isolation and nothingness, one has to examine supervoids. They are defined as vast regions in space that literally have nothing in them. In other words these have no light, no heat and no matter.

If we free ourselves from inbuilt six enemies of the mind, which are: Kama (desire), krodha (anger), lobha (greed), Mada (arrogance), moha (infatuation), and matsarya (jealousy); the negative characteristics of which bind us to the cycle of birth and death and keep it confined in this material world we will experience true isolation and nothingness.

With deep awareness, it is possible to get rid of these six enemies which I have achieved. At present I am nothing but a machine or a robot. However, in spite of knowing that I am nothing, I wanted to become something. So I asked for the third time," Narayana, I want to become Buddha; please guide me."

He said "Look, though you think that you have completely got rid of your desires and ego, you continue to aspire to become a Buddha. Having such infatuation. you start feeling emptiness again which will bring tiny cosmic elements which you call as Stars in your body, and you will continue to empty them, and you remain in this state throughout. This is one of the methods of going to Moksha or getting freedom from birth and death. But the elements in your body, the stars in your body, will remain, and some different entity will occupy them.

Gateway to Emptiness is the Lotus Sutra. This is a process in which the ego shield is removed and one gets connected with the whole Universe, and bad energies or good energies that surround the whole Universe will enter your body. You cannot manage it by meditation alone unless Gautam Buddha gives you protection. So you have to leave me now and ask for it from Buddha."

After some time, Gautam Buddha's voice reached me and said, "I am ready to take you as my disciple and give you the shield. Think it over carefully, and if you say 'Yes', and want to become a Budhha, your dedication and efforts will be far more intense". That is what happened as I reflect on it now.

Without hesitation, I said *"Yes"* to Buddha, and Buddha took over my further process and the whole process became more rigorous.

I continued with my meditation as before but with deeper intensity and for longer hours. With this level of meditation, I started experiencing further in-depth knowledge and meaning of Lotus Sutra, which earlier was not realised. My meditation process became more effective and I could explore the universe further.

With Buddha's direct guidance on Lotus Sutra, all my questions were adequately answered. Things became clear on the right path to Nirvana[15].

Narayana the Tirupati God, is a highly advanced Bodhisattva. Gautam Buddha had invited him to come down to Earth and help explain and guide in understanding Lotus Sutra. I realised that Narayana is the higher power who had been speaking to me all the time.

Introduction to Demon Guru or Demon Master

SPECULATIONS: The central core of this book is the effect of specific miraculous and strange incidents in my life which subsequently made me follow a path from 1998 till now and will continue in future.

I describe this incident: In 1992, I had a miraculous Vision. In 1994 I had a second Vision, and I continued with the advice of this Vision. While in deep meditation, I was creating Emptiness in my body and

---

15 Nirvana, the state to which all Buddhists aspire, is **the cessation of desire and hence the end of suffering**. Nirvana in Sanskrit means "the blowing out." It is understood as the extinguishment of the flame of personal desire, the quenching of the fire of life.

then going back into the creation and filling myself. I was repeatedly emptying and filling, day in and day out. But still, I had a lot of questions in my mind. I searched on the Internet for answers to those questions. I had many conversations that were happening on Spirituality on Internet forums. I also used to go for one month to the Himalayas and meet the saints there, talk to them and understand the whole process of Spirituality. During the period from 1987 to 1998, I spent a lot of time in the Himalayas.

During my journey to the Himalayas from my hometown, Pune, I had to pass through Delhi, where I had a lot of relatives and friends. Two of my friends were constantly in touch with me and, whenever we met, we shared our thoughts on our spiritual progress. Like me, they were also searching for the answers/ truths about the Universe. So whenever I went to Delhi, I met them and shared my experiences.

During one such trip, in 1995, I landed in Delhi. One of my friends was extremely excited and happy, and before I could say anything, he said he had finally met a Master. He declared that this Master was exceptional and he was the Ultimate Master. He met God; that is the way he expressed. He also felt that it would be necessary for me to go along with him to meet his Master. My search and probably my questions will also end when I meet his Master, and there may not be a need for me to go further up to the Himalayas. I was not that enthusiastic, but he persuaded me and told me he would take me in his car and drive me for 12 hrs, halfway to the Himalayas to his Master's ashram. So he offered me a free ride by car and his company. It was too alluring and I agreed. I thought even if I did not feel like accepting that Master in person, at least I would have some answers to my questions which I was trying to get in the Himalayas. So now we both proceeded in the car to the site of the ashram, where that Master was located. I stayed there for about ten days. Now I will describe the strange experiences I had during my stay there.

My first experience was: One devotee from Chandigarh who was almost my age, offered a cheque of Rs 80 lakhs to this Master. That was a considerable sum. On inquiring further, I found that he had two sons, and he felt that those two sons were useless and he would not like to give his money to them. He had decided, for better or worse, to donate all this amount to the Master who was running this ashram where he was feeding poor, orphan children and ladies who were being provided with sewing machines to sew and to earn something. He was providing food free of cost and all sorts of amenities. Though I was surprised, I appreciated that man who probably earned a lot of money and donated his money to this Master with full faith. I had also seen others giving large sums to temples and Ashrams.

The second incident that I found extremely strange. There was a big Hall, and a few ladies were sitting in that Hall for long periods, praying and singing. They did not seem to be in their senses; they were neither asleep nor awake. They were swooning; it was a very strange sight. They were doing this for six to seven days. Naturally, questions arose in my mind and I started enquiring. I was told that they come from highly respected families and are well educated and meditating. I was shocked. *What sort of meditation is this?* Naturally, I asked them more questions.

When do they go to the washroom?

When do they eat?

I asked, *"What happens during this long period?"* They said, *"Several disciples serve them, take care of them and feed them. Don't worry, they are happy. Everything is going fine, and they are in deep meditation"*.

The third incident I observed is that my friend who had brought me from Delhi to this Master was a very rich man, lived in a bungalow worth 15 to 20 crores in a very posh colony. He had only one son. He donated the upper floor of his bungalow to the Master for the sole purpose of staying whenever he came to Delhi. The friend was residing in a partly vacated part of the bungalow with his wife and son, the remaining house was for Master's disciples.

The Master had told him not to get his son married, who was of marriageable age. I asked my friend how his lineage would grow if his son was not married. He said, "No, Master has said, No marriage. So, No marriage". The reason he gave me was that his son is very good at singing and his Master liked that he developed that art. Anyhow, it was his decision.

One more thing I found strange was that my friend's wife would go inside the room of his Master, and the doors would close. Even other ladies used to go, and the doors were closed, and a disciple who might be a husband of one of the ladies would stay outside as a guard so that nobody entered that room and other husbands would be doing some Ashram work, serving, and everything. But they all would be very happy and dedicated, even the wives who were enclosed with the Master inside the room, they would think if the Master is happy, they have everything. They have got the world's wealth with them and total peace in their mind. When the ladies come out, the Master would also come out and say, *"Oh! The ladies are full of love; Cup after Cup, they feed me from their breast, and this never diminishes."* Ok, ignore that. Maybe a normal thing or an abnormal thing!! I am not here to analyze such details. How and why? Master is happy, ladies are happy, husbands are happy. Probably nothing or something spiritual is happening. So I am not going into these minor details.

Another thing I found out was that some of the devotees were afraid and reluctantly followed the path of the disciple with this Master. Some cases had been reported of suicide by the followers who refused to follow this path. This incident left a big impression on my mind. I had a personal experience with this Master, too, that the Master could communicate with me internally without speaking and even read my mind. This is a powerful Siddhi. I remember when Gautam Buddh was in search of spirituality and was looking for answers, he had met a Guru who could communicate without speaking.

I had been advised not to be impressed with such powers. My inner voice guided me. Internal, shakti of mine said, "You are not going to follow this Master. Simply speaking, there is a ghost who is under the control of this Master."

This Master had ghosts under his control. This ghost would read your mind. He would feed the questions to the Master, the Master would give back the answer to the ghost, and the ghost would put it back in your mind. I was satisfied with the explanation.

This Master would collect a few disciples and take all of us to a nearby Christian or Muslim Cremation ground. It was in an Army area. He would make us sit in that area and ask us to meditate. The Graveyard, Kabristaan, further convinced me that, usually, ghosts are supposed to exist in that area, and **I, as a practitioner of Emptiness,** could feel their heavy energies roaming around. But I was not afraid.

Then, another incident happened. I didn't want to move out of my room to a place where that Master was giving Satsang, but my body did not obey me. I was forced physically, lifted off my feet, and had to go to his place. It was a great incident of losing control of your body. You cannot guide/control your movements of the body, and you find yourself helpless. But never mind. Once again, my experience of meditation clearly showed me that there was a ghost inside my body which was very powerful, who was not allowing me to control my body, rather, he was in command of my body. I used my awareness in understanding this subtle negative energy of the ghosts, permeating my mind and stalling it. It gave me extraordinary confidence that my Shakti was working inside me, and I had returned to Poona. Inmates and disciples of ashram could not believe that the friend of a true and dedicated disciple of Master had escaped and had not agreed to become Master's disciple.

Limited Emptiness

Inside me, the Shakti told me that this Master is a Master of Ghosts and his sister, also a ghost (accomplice) lives in Hell. This sister, power of Darkness and the brother, who is now in the human body, both control a huge number of ghosts, Pisach-Hungry ghost, in Hell. This Master, in this body, captures certain souls who are not good, weak-minded, not learned, and makes them ghosts with the help of his sister and makes use of them in their evil deeds.

Those disciples who helped the Ashram and donated sums for the welfare of the Ashram, to feed poor ladies, children and men, they loved the cause of creation. Master helps them, saves them, and also goes to the extent of protecting them from outside elements. So the disciples who, out of total devotion to their Master, surrender their properties, surrender their families, including their wives and children, to the Master. They are totally happy because they have surrendered everything of theirs to Master, including themselves and their 'I consciousness'. They feel that whatever is happening to them is because of the Master. They feel the Master in them. They are in **limited Emptiness** because of their devotion to their Master, and they go on doing for good causes. Good Causes earn them Good Karmas. Their lives in general, when they return to their respective homes, would be very healthy, happy and prosperous. They prosper further and despite that, if something wrong happens, the Master protects them. What more do they want? They have everything. This is the way these disciples worship and lead their life. They were happy when they were in the Ashram. They are happy when they are at home doing earthly duties.

Here my friend told me about another incident and how the Master protects them in the world. He said that once he had filed Income tax returns with some error and the Income Tax department sent him a Notice, and he was totally disturbed because he knew he could be penalized. So when he received notice from the government office, he requested his Master, in meditation, "Master, I am in trouble; please protect me," Master told him not to worry and assured him that he would take care of him. He went to the Income Tax office. As narrated by my friend...

The officer who was handling his case called him. They were sitting opposite each other. Officer called for the file related to my friend's Return Documents. When the file came, Officer opened it, and my friend could see his Returns paper, but the officer was not able to locate it. He kept on searching for the document. Then he got an urgent phone call from his boss. So he left the file on the table, and went to meet his boss. My friend had seen the paper, but the officer did not see it. My friend kept praying to the Master for protection.

My friend said...

"The officer returned after meeting his boss. His mind was preoccupied with some other issue. He was feeling a little at a loss". He told my friend, "Please come again when I call you. I cannot locate your papers. I'm too busy. Come next time". He did not call again. That matter got finished there. This is how the Masters protect the disciples.

Of course, my shakti told me this was very simple. When my friend saw the document in the file, his mind said. This is the paper.

The Master immediately sent a ghost, who was instrumental in the phone call, and the officer moved away from his seat. The friend quietly removed it.The matter was handled smoothly. These are the strange incidents I was coming across, and searching for reasonings and truth all the time.

Ghosts were obeying their Master, a Spirit who was a lady, and her brother who was a Master in human life. They were both managing the Ashram of human beings on Earth & Ghost World, giving strength to each other and expanding their Empire. And these ghosts were ready to sacrifice their interest and follow the their Master's order and they were also gaining.

Look at this amazing situation. Master is prospering, and his sister, who is again a controller of Dark forces in Hell, is prospering. The Ghosts who are bearing their Karmas and suffering when they come to my body are also prospering. They are going to Emptiness and going for rebirth. Where is the loss? There is no loss anywhere.

This method of that Ghost Master, sister and brother Human Master together because of the powers they had gained by using partly good Karma accumulation method and partly a bad Karma accumulation method were prospering in the right combination.

Some of his devotees told me that one person who refused to accept the Master's teachings committed suicide later on. My friend from Delhi also told me about an incident that showed me how these powers could be used by the master to control human beings around him. He may be using these powers for the good of the people because he was taking away money from the rich and helping the poor. His intentions may be good, but basically, he was the one **deciding the fate of his devotees.** The disciple loses his freedom of thinking and action. My friend from Delhi was a wealthy man, and all his wealth was being utilized for the facilities at the Ashram. He had also lost control over his son, who was not allowed to marry, and his wife would always give priority to the Master. My friend told me when his Master called him, he would make it a point to reach the Master's house at the earliest by driving 12 hours at a stretch and leaving all his work behind. My friend worshiped the Master as God.

That was too much. I wanted to live in freedom, without fear or fun for any reason. I did not wish to be controlled by such Ghost Masters. I was totally convinced with my meditation methods of Emptiness, which I followed, though it had many uncertainties. I walked out of the Ashram. This incident gave me the confidence to continue with my meditation because I knew I was achieving something extraordinary. I could get out of the clutches of such a Master.

It was like a big victory, and I would talk about it, showcasing myself as a hero and that Master as a villain. Somehow, this news must have reached that

Master, through my friend, who was angry. During my visits to Delhi thereafter, whenever I met him, he expressed his resentment at my reaction to the visit to that evil Master. I was steady in my opinion about that Master which I used to express but my friend continued with his devotion to his Master.

Tragedy Strikes

Ten years had passed since I walked out from that Evil Master's Ashram. In the year 2005, I had a surprise visit from two ladies to my Pune residence. These were the ladies I had seen in Master's Ashram who were singing and swaying for hours and days together. I was indeed surprised but welcomed the uninvited guests.

These ladies stayed with us for one day. They asked me for my daughter Gita's address, who lived in Aundh, Pune and I gave the address to them.

Gita or Gitu was beautiful, spirited, joyful, extrovert, enthusiastic, and a darling to everyone. She was a brilliant child and had received Gold Medal in M.E. and LifeTime Achievement Award as the best Engineering Teacher. She was loved, liked, and adored by family, friends, and students.

These ladies met Gitu and spent some time at her house. I was not able to think much, I was confused, but subsequently, a few dangerous things happened. My daughter started getting highly disturbed. I now realize that the disturbance was because of some ghost energy that had entered her body and had unstabilized her.

Gita talked about the ladies among other things and started getting weaker by the day. This continued for a month and a half. And one day, she was ill with Dengue and she died. It was 7th Nov 2005 a very tragic day for us as gloom and despair descended on us. But things did not end at that . My daughter was not the enemy of that Ashram; I was the Enemy. My mind was fuddled and confused. I could not think of meditating even for one second in that situation. Taking advantage of my mental condition, a powerful ghost entered my body. He created a situation where I fell from a ladder and broke my spine.

The fracture to the spine was severe and the pain excruciating. I was in a hopeless state. Most probably, the ghost was trying to kill me. After two to three days of visiting the doctor, an encouraging voice suddenly spoke to me. "Come on; You are greater than you think. The pain that the doctors say won't subside for months must be ignored. The power is within you; sit still and meditate with awareness on it. You can control the pain. Don't get disheartened. You can manage your health". The voice within gave me extraordinary power to go deep into meditation, and I noticed that the pain started reducing within 2-3 days. It was a remarkable incident for me. Remarkable in a bad and a good way. It was bad in the sense that I lost my daughter and good that I had been on the path, which is very powerful and good, better than that of the Master who could read your mind using ghosts. and controlled your life. At least it has something more than that.

The War Begins

The biggest struggle and the most dangerous period in my life was when my daughter passed away in 2005. I have tears in my eyes remembering and talking about her even today. My daughter went through an immense struggle and I went through severe pain myself in the struggle to help her. Divinity must have given me this role to play. It did not matter to me whether I succeeded or failed.

Gitu/ Upasana Matnani died of Dengue - Advance Shock syndrome within two days of its detection at the time of the Diwali festival. She was just 38 years old and the favorite professor of her students in the Engineering College. We did not realize the severity of her illness. Doctors, too, weren't readily available as it was the festival season. By the time it was diagnosed, her body was swollen, and the next day she passed away.

When someone is born, the exit point in their life is decided, and depending on the creativity/ wisdom level of the person, their Sword sharpens, and life lengthens. Buddha's main aim was to end old age, misery, suffering and ill health.

In Gitus' death, many factors played a role. Her Karmas, her Creative level, until that point, her mental and physical health all mattered. I will explain some details after giving the background of how the Universe/ Creator works.

The Master had declared war on me. He killed my daughter, and he tried to kill me. And now I know this was destined to happen. In the previous Yug, we had been fighting each other without reaching the end result, and in this Yug again, the same cycle continued. Going to him through my Delhi friend was destined, so it happened. I had just recovered from the death blow, also broke my back, and had come out stronger with greater faith in Lotus Sutra, which I was following and worshipping and reading the book and trying to understand further and meditate. Almost day and night, I was spending time on Lotus Sutra, with the hope that I would learn methods by which I can win over suffering, diseases, pain, death, etc., which are a curse for humanity.

In this search for the method, unfortunately, I had reached out to this Master, who was an influential ghost leader. He had an army of ghosts under him, all types of ghosts, small, big, good, dangerous, very dangerous, and he had declared war on me for a minor reason that I did not accept him.

The basic idea is that a person comes to life and dies. When he dies, his Karmas which are not yet ripe, start ripening between the Zone of Death & Next life. If the

Karmas are negative, the person concerned suffers from the pain of Hell. And if the Karmas are strongly negative, he remains in that Zone for a very long time and considers his survival on remaining a Ghost and **then he starts poaching on other lives.**

Chapter 5

"I now rejoice and have no fear, And among the Bodhisattvas,
I shall cast expedients aside and be straightforward,
Speaking only of the supreme Path." [16]

Introduction to Lokas

16 Supreme path (courtesy): http://www.cttbusa.org/lotus/lotus_contents.asp.html (refer Appendix pg xxxii)

It was the beginning of 1994 when I was introduced to the higher path of the role of Kalki. Our Earth in plane number 26, is connected to some 8 to 10 Lokas. All these Lokas have to be eliminated. In the book of *A Collection Commemorating the Teaching of Sayagi U Ba Khin,* it talks about Lokas.

These Lokas are not desirable but were created due to necessity. Hell and Heaven are not required. A simple term used for *Hell & Heaven* is Loka. These Lokas were created because of the inhabitants' ignorance who indulged in more wrong Karmas which they could not clear in the same birth which resulted in forced carry forward. During the transit period between two births they get located in applicable Lokas and there they face consequences of their Karmas. *In lower Lokas they take the sufferings for Bad Karmas that they had accumulated and then in higher Lokas they enjoy peace and tranquility*. These bad Karmas, as well as some good Karmas which they had accumulated result in their settlement in applicable Lokas to clear at least part of such Karmas. Accumulation of Karmas, which all individuals do in their life of existence and elimination of this process is the first work that a Kalki has to do.

10 Lokas connected with Earth[17] 3 Broad divisions of Lokas[18]

Six Deva Lokas

Catumaharajika
Tavatimsa
Yama
Tusita
Nimmanarati
Paranimmita-vasavatti

The Human World

The four Lower Worlds

Niraya (hell)
Tricchana (animal world)
Peta (ghost world)
Asura (demon world)

(Courtesy :The division of the Universe as per , *A Collection Commemorating The Teaching of Sayagi U Ba Khin* mentioning the different Lokas.)

When Kalki comes to Earth he dissolves these Lokas. Kalki needs these qualities or Kalaas (Hindi word means Art). He has to acquire skills to handle

---

17 6 Upper Lokas and 4 Lower Lokas are connected with Earth

18 3 broad divisions of these Lokas (Courtesy: https://co.pinterest.com/pin/640988959438618179/)

(Courtesy https://www.google.com/imgres?imgurl=https://i.pinimg.com/originals/ed/f3/c7/edf3c74efaad0dc43923ed2903a07d83.jpg&imgrefurl=https://www.pinterest.com/pin/735705289103270121/&tbnid=Ol_t648R_TekkM&vet=1&docid=5UUASAztuKZQRM&w=1080&h=1350&hl=en-GB&source=sh/x/im)

Pishachas[19], Demons and pass through this complex painful process. A human has to be trained to face them to prepare him for his spiritual evolution.

As I mentioned earlier, I was attacked by the ghost after having experienced the effects of negative energies in my life and body and the danger to life from them. When my daughter died, I could not locate her quickly because she was taken away by the ghost to deep regions. I was angry and felt helpless. I had the Power of Lotus Sutra; I developed strong willpower to locate and destroy this dangerous zone as much as Lotus Sutra wanted to do. So in a way, I was firmly attached to Lotus Sutra because I was a *Soldier of Lotus Sutra in the previous Era*, and the same is repeated in this birth. The fight is on, and the fight is intense.

For the past 28 years since 1994, unconsciously, I had accepted Lotus Sutra, and the fight had been predetermined. Every day I would enter the Zone of Hell and return. Then I started going twice or thrice a day inside the Hell zone and returning after cleansing as many demons as possible. In this fight, I had been slowly damaging my body. I had war scars on my body. Both my eyes were damaged. I could hardly see, and doctors made some mistakes because of the powerful effect of ghosts. My gallbladder had become nonfunctional. My heart had become weak. I had developed an infection in my stomach. Also, along

---

19Courtesy : (ref Pg 65 of Lotus Sutra book)

with these disorders, I developed a urinary problem. So each moment of my life was agony by the time I reached 80. Every moment was torture because of wounds or scars incurred during fighting in hell. But I was determined and not worried about pain, suffering, or even death. I had to fight because they had taken away my daughter.

Then one day my son, (in the year 2017) had to admit me to the hospital for treatment and operations. The Doctors kept me in the hospital for a couple of days. They checked all my parameters and said, *"We can not operate on this person due to old age and other complications. He has a lot of problems in his body. We can only advise giving him painkillers. Take him home, and give him painkillers. To keep him happy, make his life as enjoyable as possible"*. I, too, insisted that I would not like to die in the hospital; I would rather die at home. That night I was brought back home. I was in terrible pain. And it was overwhelming. It was trying to kill my awareness.

The Divine Message

As long as I was aware, I was fighting and wanted to die fighting. But if my awareness went away, then these enemies in my body causing me suffering would also take me away to a place where recovery would be impossible. I would be lost forever. And that was a great agony in my mind. Not only would I lose the war, but I would also not be able to come back in the future to continue the war.

I felt that higher Gods had deceived me. I asked Higher Gods,

"Why have you deceived me?".

"I was to die in awareness, and here I am dying in absolute pain, losing all awareness. And if this is happening, then you are deceivers. You are cheaters."

And most probably, I died. I say I died because I went through a very strange situation that could happen after death and can also happen in a dream.

The scene that happened was extremely vivid and unforgettable. At the end of this heavenly scene and discussion, I was asked to return to Earth and live again to continue with my unfinished task. I was assured that I would not only start recovering but would become better daily. I felt better when I woke up, and I remembered that dream. It may be a vision. I considered it a vision and have noted it in my diary and my record for the future. It was a very, very strange dream. I did not dare to say anything to anybody. But after one week or so, I recovered sufficiently to sit in the balcony. Taking my son Sunil into confidence, I narrated my dream in some detail and asked for his views.

"Look, I am still alive. I had this Vision. I am not taking any medicines. What is your view?" After thinking Sunil said to me,

"Papa, I cannot say whether your vision was real or just a dream. Let us wait. We will know the answers after a month or so."

Inner Voice & Visions

I died or probably went to sleep. I am not sure. If I died, it was a vision. If I went to sleep, it would be a dream. But now, when I look back, approximately six years later, I think it was a vision. I had indeed died. What I saw was astonishing.

I saw an infinite God in space. Below him, there were two platforms. One was a little higher than the other. At the higher platform were a few 100 grey-clothed human beings and at the lower platform, there were white-robed human beings. Between these two platforms stood a tall figure, a leader-like personality.

I was brought into the scene and the voice of God boomed.

"He has a complaint. He wants to die in awareness with the help of the Lotus Sutra. Yet he was losing awareness''.

The leader in question rose and spoke,

"We had provided him with 5th level Protection".

God's voice boomed again,

"Wrong, he should have been provided with Zero level Protection; he has to go back to complete his unfinished task" and then the whole scene disappeared.

Later I sat in meditation, analyzed and asked many questions for clarity. I was advised to stop taking all medication and I would recover. I would live a healthy life and my work would be easier and smoother due to the higher level of protection I would get. I immediately stopped taking all painkiller medicines that doctors prescribed. My health improved considerably. The Zero-level protection was sufficient to keep me from extreme dangers when I went to hell to fight with negative entities, ghosts, etc. My work became easier and smoother. In one of my photos in this book(on the next page), taken recently you can always see a Green Orb surrounding me for Protection, which I assume is the PROTECTION I have received.

Yet I was getting weaker by the day. I was persistently asked by my family to stop the cleansing process in my meditation. But I preferred to continue shining and extending the Sword of Lotus Sutra as long as I was alive. I wanted to do my best in this era as much as possible.

I continued the process till age 85, and each time I got weaker despite protection. One day I fell and hurt myself badly and thought my end had come. I felt happy that I had done my maximum and would die in complete awareness. I could continue in my next birth.

But no! I was not to die. I recovered from that incident and heard an inside Voice saying, *"You have accumulated enough,* ***Jhanas***[20]*. Now go and use your Sword of Lotus Sutra on a flying Horse of Emptiness in your body and work as a Kalki in this era till you die. You are going to live for another 25 years."*

I was taken aback. Another 25 years? One moment I felt I wouldn't be alive for another day and here I was being told that I would live for another 25 years!!!

A Green Orb on my left-hand side can be seen. It represents that I have Healing and Protection Angel by my side at all times.

---

20 Refer Appendix pg xlii

Well, I do not know whether this will happen, but now I fight like an expert soldier and always come back victorious. With Zero level protection around me, I feel safe. My health is improving. I might live that long, and this work will continue. I have moved from a dangerous state of pain and suffering to a superlative state of power, peace, and prosperity.

This process of extending the sword of Lotus Sutra is creating more Jhanas (Wisdom/ Antivirus system) in my body. Each time I came across a negative entity of a different type, it required a fight with different skills to clean that Energy. The repeated effort has created Wisdom in my body and the work has become automatic.

Strategy of The Lotus Sutra

Meditation of Emptiness cannot happen unless you first go to the Death zone in your meditation. When I sit in meditation, I see heavy Karmas in my astral body through pain, suffering and extremely painful vibrations. This is the portion I call Hell in my body.

When I die, or when my time comes, I will not have the support of my body, and these same Karmas will cause me additional suffering. That's what I refer to as going through Hell after Death.

Similarly, when I lose myself every day in meditation of Emptiness, heavy Karmas get released first, followed by light Karmas, which are pleasant. These are a result of good deeds in my life. That portion is gratifying and I call it Heaven.

Whether meditating or not, after death every person goes to hell first. It is always better to clear your Karmas while in the physical body. *The support of the body helps make the suffering mild as one can divert the mind through friends, entertainment, or medicines.* This helps one suffer partly as per the body's tolerance capacity and store the remaining suffering for later.

After Death, this is not possible, and if the suffering is heavy, he goes through Hell. Once the negative karmas are exhausted, he moves on to Heaven to enjoy and exhaust positive karmas. After exhausting his karmas, he returns to the source where he started his journey as a Soul. There he recuperates, learns from the experience of Hell & Heaven, stores those learnings in the body as *Wisdom*, and then gets into the cycle of birth again.

During the initial years of meditating, when I had asked the higher power that I wanted to become the Buddha. I was told the Path is challenging. The reason was my Ego shield was broken and removed. Now I meditate without the shield. Losing myself in meditation every day, I go into the Zone where dead souls exist. *Millions of life in this existence die, and they are in the Hell Zone of togetherness. I go through that Zone and some of those Spirits who are unable to bear their suffering see the Emptiness in me and occupy my Empty space. I am like water, which cools them in the burning fire. The shield of my body saves them. [21]These Souls come back to me, back in life as a part of my life.* This is how I take away the heavy sufferings of ghosts, Spirits and strongly negative people.

Through the process of my meditation, I clean those energies. These Karmas of mine are stored in the ***Sambhog Kaya, Kaya of Karmas.*** These Sambhog Kaya Karmas along with its benefits can be taken back by the same Spirit to its next life when it is reborn.

This happens to human beings all the time. You must have seen some people come into our lives. They do good to us and leave without taking any rewards for their action, whereas some come into our lives offering

21 Sometimes, author writes as an individual and some other occasions he writes as Kalki. This para refers to Kalki's statement, Once helped by Kalki, the Atmas return to him even in next births as they know that Kalki is the one who can relieve them from Karmas.

us only pain and suffering and leave. All these are *Sambhog Kaaya Karmas.*

My work is mainly in Hell. Bear in mind that I cannot help Spirits unless they agree to be helped or come to me of their own will. A Spirit of a dead person that cannot bear the suffering any more enters my body to be healed. Sometimes the Spirits are afraid of being hurt, but when they see another Spirit healed, they are tempted to enter my body. Initially, very few Spirits dared to enter my body because they feared the outcome, though they were suffering a lot. But now, I have become popular in Hell; in a sense, many Spirits wait for my visit, and when they see me coming, they rush to occupy the Empty space in my body.

It is good that the portion that is Hell, the partition that is beyond this body, has a connective hell that is intensely reducing. *The delay of playing Karma in Hell is reducing as these energies are getting lesser.*

Some of the Spirits were very dangerous and beyond my power to be cleansed and saved as my wisdom was limited. As I mentioned earlier, initially, I was given 5th level protection assuming that my emptiness could go only up to the 5th level of awareness. Still, later on, when I had that Vision at the age of 80, God pointed out the mistake and I was given Zero level protection. The Emptiness level in me being all-powerful led to the shield being immensely strong, and I could encounter the most dangerous Spirits, which could otherwise have harmed me permanently. I was not supposed to suffer from the ill health of my Gallbladder, Stomach, Eyes, Ears, Teeth, Urine, and Stomach infections. A mistake led to my suffering.

Now with the Zero-level protection, I am safe and healthy. My body is now recovering from the effects of the ill health that I had accumulated. My meditation weakens its effect. I am growing younger and better in my daily activities.

Tulsidas, of Sri Ramcharitrmanas, went to Moksh to meet God because he was a devotee of Rama. I never went for Moksh because when I tasted the Emptiness, I knew I did not exist, *so where is the question of getting Moksh, if I don't exist?* The notion that I EXIST, is false. I am a Maya or Illusion. *But this Illusion is very powerful. This Maya causes pain and suffering as well happiness and creates Karmas.*

Luckily, Lotus Sutra, in the first chapter, also agrees with me that *whoever asks for Moksha or goes to God is a wasted energy. But when he becomes Arahant, he contributes to the objective of God which is the Creation with Wisdom. He does not want to escape the existence that is created by God, which is just an Illusion*. It doesn't help the system.

Lotus Sutra deals with the system. It started millions of years ago and found the loopholes in the creation of this existence. This existence was supposed to be creative, but in reality, it was also accumulating very wrong things, like negative and positive emotional energies, which did not help in building up wisdom oriented creativity. *Lotus Sutra came into existence to remove this wasteful energy. It is a sort of filtration system that cleans a body that has accumulated positive and negative emotional energies.*

It extracts the negative energies of an individual which is taken by my Sambhog Kaya. These negative energies are processed and resulting positive energies are given back to the person so that he can again use them for Creativity.

Now to analyse the Master.

This Master is a product of negative emotions-negative energies.

That means the system had gone so bad on our Earth that not only did negative energies get accumulated, but also created powerful Masters who tried to keep these negative energies alive and continued to expand them.

After giving wide credence to the Wisdom of Lotus Sutra, I went after this whole negative system of creation. We do not require ghosts or Masters of Ghosts or Hell. These negative systems are unnecessarily overloading God's Creativity.

In the process of massive creation stretching wide horizons we have gone through unfortunate circumstances and failures. What we have learned is how it has major repercussions on the Universe, and mending/ repairing these unfortunate errors takes millions of years.

In Kaliyug, many people want to gain immediate wealth, position, fame, and love by extracting others' Karmas that otherwise were never theirs. This is a grave issue . The more they extract, the more they get addicted to enjoying and exalting and causing others immense pain and suffering and miseries. Once they get hold of some ghost or Spirit (through Tantriks, Maulvis, Aghoras) they could command, they create havoc and destruction in families they are in contact with. They first try to influence the head of the family, and as everyone listens to the head, it becomes easy for that greedy person to control, influence and destroy anyone in that family. Divorces, death, anger issues, domestic abuse, health issues, and misunderstandings are deepened, with no respite of ever healing, and the gap widens never to unite anyone.

The person who is influenced, cannot see beyond his own selfish needs and does not bother about others including his own family. He has no time to talk nicely to anyone in his family. He waits earnestly on the influencer, wasting his time till he is permitted to entertain or be with that greedy person, who treats him like dirt.

The influenced person, reports all family matters and talks on every aspect of his family. The greedy person creates an attractive aura / shield around himself to lure weak minds. Having a weak mind he feels nice about it as somebody has time **to listen to his intelligent views on every issue.** The greedy person takes the information to further manipulate to his advantage and calls on Spirits to make matters worse for the family. Promotions long due get stuck up and good news cannot be tolerated by the greedy person, and he strikes major health emergencies to let the money flow out and create tensions in the family.

The sad part is that the head of the family never thinks or accepts the fact that he was under the influence of any one from outside, due to the Spirits who manipulate and control his mind in favour of their Master. Spirit also creates destructive, negative thoughts in the victim. Clothes, nails, hair, or even the dust of his feet is used by the evil masters as a media to influence and impose control of his body and mind. Such masters use the hungry Spirits to achieve their goal to make the victim fall under the bad influence of lust, power, and property. Even water from such manipulative masters with mantras chanted can kill someone!!!

There are thousands of such manipulative people now in Kaliyug and this Yug is overloaded and the gap between Hell and Heaven is increasing tremendously. The greedy person initially enters the house, through the weakness the poor influencer might have, concerning Kaam, Krodh, lobh. Once the GREEDY PERSON has given his/her body and time even once, the head of the family feels forever obliged to serve the

USELESS PERSON, not knowing it has been done by commanding the Spirit world.

This causes a major tilt in the Universe, Hell, and Heaven.

Some GREEDY, useless people even go to the extent of deciding the destiny of others and killing them/ their family in the process and do not feel remorseful about it. They want to play God and create fear in the minds of people. One subtitle in the index should be: ***WHO gave YOU the authority to change Our Karma?*** Mostly the person who does this will be your very close relative or friend who holds long-standing grudges and feels elated after quietly destroying you and your family. If some family still survives through these issues, it is due to a highly advanced soul born or chaste bride entering the household, who is aware and forever remains as a guard to protect the family.

God does not interfere in our part of creation directly or indirectly. He comes down only through birth as Avatars and those are few and far between. He creates systems after being born as an Avatar and gives a boost to the system that pushes the evolution forward.

Lotus Sutra also came as a system to clean some mistakes that creation was making. We are supposed to be creative ***(Nirmaan Kaya)*** beings with wisdom. Nirmaan Kaya & Dharam Kaya's combination does not create a weak system; it is big enough to benefit many Souls. That is called ***Sambhog Kaya.***

Everything else that we are doing is a waste of energy. Emotions such as hate, anger, fear, love, etc., unnecessarily accumulate in our bodies and are a burden to us. They cause diseases and suffering. Not only that, these accumulated emotions gain intelligence to take more and more of our life energy into them to survive. Then they become very dangerous negative entities in our body. We create ghosts in our bodies too.

That is why it is important to understand the system. When you try to understand and rectify this system, you come across **Lotus Sutra.** This creation is trillions of years old. The negative energies were simple when it was at a very high level. Lotus Sutra came into existence around the same time. It has grown with this creation as well.

As the creation expands, enormous problems come with it. Lotus Sutra expands accordingly. **The SWORD of Kalki** is getting longer and stronger as per the requirement. The creation is moving ahead, and its negative aspects are also moving ahead, but the system God created in the form of the Lotus Sutra is also evolving and extending to purify the system.

The Kalki effect on our Earth grows with time, along with the power of the Lotus Sutra. **Lotus Sutra is the Sword of Kalki.** The effect and power of the Lotus Sutra grows when we add ***Jhanas (Wisdom body, anti-virus system) t***o it. I have been adding *Jhanas* to my body since 1994. Creating each Jhana in my body cost me a lot of suffering. I would go to the Emptiness in meditation and then enter Hell. There I would collect a vicious ghost in extreme pain and suffering who would willingly enter my body to get relief from suffering. Those pains would enter my body, and then in meditation, I would create or strengthen the Jhanas.

Chapter 6

"In the Beginning, there was Emptiness."

Lotus Sutra, The Ultimate Weapon

Twenty-Five hundred years ago, Gautam Buddha uttered the Lotus Sutra. In that era, there was no system of writing, so he said it in the form of lyrics. He said whatever he has learned about Sutras, Lotus Sutra is most important. Lotus Sutra is at the highest level and one of the foremost knowledge one can seek. There are numerous Mahayana Sutras, more than twenty four approximately of which *Saddharmapundarīka-sūtra (Lotus Sutra) is the most venerated.*

This complete Lotus Sutra is sung compulsorily in all Mahayana temples.. This Sutra takes some 2.5 to 3 hours to be sung. When scriptures started to be written, it was first written in either Pali or Sanskrit. Then it was translated in multiple languages. The first translation was in Chinese. In this century or a century back, an American University sanctioned a project in which a Committee was formed to translate this Sutra into English.

I have read this Lotus Sutra by author Burton Watson. Any translation cannot be cent percent correct because Lotus Sutra's knowledge is so deep that no one can understand it entirely, and every word has to be appropriately weighed. That's why the Committee was formed and meditation experts, Chinese experts, and Americans all sat together to translate it. Yet, it can not be said precisely that it is 100% accurate.

I have seen it still being sung in Mahayana temples by 200 to 300 devotees with drums.

For Two thousand years, this custom has been carried forward, and this is sung in thousands of Temples even today . If we calculate, lakhs of person-hours have been spent singing it. It is also said that this Sutra, written in Golden letters on the Golden cover, is displayed all over Mahayana temples in prominent places to create awareness of the importance of this holy book among visitors and devotees.

Christ's followers wrote the Bible, the Prophet created the Koran, Gurunanak delivered Guru Granth Sahib, and believers worship these Granths. Similarly, Lotus Sutra is worshipped; the only difference is that people easily read and understand the Bible, Koran and Guru Granth Sahib, and devotees follow the Path. *But the Lotus Sutra is such that it is hardly ever understood even today.* Gautam Buddha has said that the birth of the Lotus Sutra took place millions of years back. Over the years, understanding it has become vague and difficult due to the extended time between its Creation and the present era. Secondly, it is written that life is more vast and extensive than we know, and Spirits exist in different planes. Hence understanding it is extremely difficult, and thus it is only worshipped.

When I came to know of Lotus Sutra, I got the book. I started reading and became crazy about it. I read a few pages, understood some 10% of it, and found that knowledge wonderful and of great value.

I thought I could catch hold of disciples or people who have gone through Lotus Sutra and joined Discussion forums. Still, after many hours of sitting on the Internet and talking, sharing discussions for many years with many Buddha disciples and people all over the world who had this knowledge, I finally concluded that they knew very little. They didn't want to talk about it. They feared talking because it has been said in Lotus Sutra that anyone who deciphers the wrong meaning of Lotus Sutra will be harmed or punished very severely. So many didn't want to get into the depth of the Lotus Sutra. it was only worshipped.

In 2012, I openly shared my views, and people abused me and condemned me. I wish to forget such incidents. I couldn't understand that people worldwide were singing and worshipping for so many years without understanding the Lotus Sutra. Then *why the heck did Gautam Buddha talk about Lotus Sutra? Who would have benefited from reading and understanding this Lotus Sutra?"*

But now, after realizing it, I see myself reaping the benefits of it over the years. After understanding it and practically walking on the Path , I feel that even if one person understands it after 2000 years, then the importance of it is so great that he can compensate for it. Let's see what happens next, in future.

One more thing about Lotus Sutra is that it stores millions of years of wisdom and knowledge in it. Like in a computer, when we click a key, we get answers to many years of people's understanding and the truth buried in it. So there is no doubt you can get correct answers if you *connect* to it, brushing aside assumptions and ignorance.

One of the mantra in it says:

ALL BUDDHAS PAST, PRESENT, AND FUTURE
ABIDE IN **EMPTINESS** AND
FOLLOW THE PATH OF **ONE VEHICLE**.

Now some words are most important in this.

EMPTINESS- the experience of two years in emptiness for me is probably said to be Arahant by Hindus. Until you reach the stage of emptiness, you cannot understand anything. You cannot even touch the book of Lotus Sutra. So I reached that stage of emptiness after two years of my rigorous meditation process. But we Hindus, after reaching the stage of emptiness, yearn for Mukti, Moksh, i.e., try to free ourselves from the birth and death cycle; we talk about it.

To understand, connect or benefit from Lotus Sutra, it is essential to experience emptiness (Arahant) in meditation. Whichever Buddhas have come in the past and will come in the present or future have to connect with emptiness first. That is the gate to the entry of Lotus Sutra.

Once the connection is established, ***One Vehicle*** path of the Lotus Sutra can be followed. What does that mean? It means that we follow the Lotus Sutra in totality and start getting guidance in all our decisions and actions. As the link strengthens, we get in-depth knowledge and then we perform according to the guidance.

There is no surrendering to the Lotus Sutra. One has to experience Emptiness, which is a *gateway to enter Lotus Sutra.* Let us say if one is in fear. he should sit in awareness meditation and know the fear. He can counter it with many types of wisdom.

1. It will pass away.

2. Nothing is permanent.

3. At the most, I will die, so let it be.

4. Fear is not a solution.

5. I admit that I am in fear, so what.

6. God/Guru/ Lotus Sutra/ Buddha is with me. etc.

And then, one should feel emptiness, and when fear energy has faded away, one should repeat this process again and again till it becomes automatic. Now it becomes a Jhana-ANTIVIRUS SYSTEM. This is a gate of entry to the Lotus Sutra. This gate of wisdom is now a part of your body and mind. One is now connected to the Lotus Sutra.

One has to make many such connections. Say for hate, greed, love, sex, etc. Each gate will give you benefits of some kind. This is the only way to grow and become a God or a Buddha. Devotion is a reverse method. One does not grow in devotion. One should strengthen wisdom. Each wisdom is a gate for Lotus Sutra. We were told earlier that Arahant or Emptiness is the end of our journey. One becomes free from the cycle of birth and death. Lotus sutra says, *"No. It is the beginning of the process of gaining wisdom."*

Anyone who wishes to become Buddha has to rise above this world of duality. This is the only path, the only vehicle to cross samsara/ life. Lotus Sutra helps one to rise above ignorance and thereby, ends the suffering. Wisdom and good health are its by-products.

People then would think to themselves, why not live in harmony and peace and this dream of the enlightenment of the human race was stated in Chapter 16 of the Sutra, in the so-called Great Desire:

at all times, I think to myself,
how can I cause all people
to attain enlightenment to the Buddha's way
(of living in harmony and peace).

Lotus Sutra and Gautam Buddha never commented on God. When asked, he said neither Yes nor No, for God.

Secondly, the Lotus Sutra denies the existence of Atma, while our Upanishads[22] say that Atma exists for human beings. ***The third significant difference was Lotus Sutra mentions that Arahant as a DOOR to access the source which also rectifies the flaws in the Existence, which is full of Pain, Suffering and Death.*** In my meditation, I have asked many questions about the differences.

Naturally, if I want answers, Buddhism was very clear about Atma, God, Arahant, or Emptiness. These answers had come from God Himself. Some changes happened in me some three-four years back, and I started getting answers to these differences.

In Fact, as per the Vedas, these differences are due to some conditions, and they do not make Buddhism separate from the Vedas.

Puranas[23] believe that the 9th Avatar was Buddha. Buddha did not comment on God, while Vedas talk

---

22 Vedantic Upanishad describes three types of Self (atman): the Bahya-atma or external self (body), the Antar-atma or inner self (individual soul) and the Param-atma or highest self (the Brahman, Purusha). (refer Appendix pg xlvi- Atma Upanishad)

(Courtesy: https://en.wikipedia.org/wiki/Atma_Upanishad#:~:text=It%20is%20classified%20as%20a%20Samanya%20(general)%20and%20Vedantic%20Upanishad.&text=The%20Upanishad%20describes%20three%20types,(the%20Brahman%2C%20Purusha).

23 (courtesy) The Buddha was integrated into Vaishnavism through its mythology in the Vaishnava Puranas, Buddha is adopted as the ninth avatar of Vishnu. https://en.wikipedia.org/wiki/Gautama_Buddha_in_Hinduism#:~:text=The%20Buddha%20was%20integrated%20into,the%20devas%20in%20their%20battles.

about God as an Entity that never diminishes nor increases, and everything comes out of God. Anything that comes out of God separates from God as a newborn gets separated from the womb of the mother, and it has its own sphere of action. But the higher God's awareness can draw back that, which was created by subdivision.

So this process has continued, and God came to a certain level of Division. After which I think, a word which comes is ***MAYA- Illusion.*** I think Maya/ Illusion and Emptiness are one and the same thing. It's like a Shadow of God or an image of God.

MAYA- Emptiness: This has the same properties as Gods. But remember it is Shadow of God, not the God from where different Gods came. So we assume that this creation came from Maya or Shadow of God.

Even the Lotus Sutra describes its birth after Sun-Moon-Bright (in Chapter 1, Introduction pg 14)[24], came into existence. Before that, Lotus Sutra did not exist. So if we assume that Buddhas arose from the Shadow or Maya of God, then naturally, Buddhas cannot comment on God because they cannot reach the same level as God. Similarly, a subdivided God can be called Atma because each of these Atmas or subdivided Gods started their own creation in their own way and the head of that creation was Brahma of that area. So that

---

24 Courtesy (ref Pg 14 of LS book)

becomes an Atma. So God's image, which started this creation, also comes below it.

Naturally, Gautam Buddha or his ancestors Buddha who came because of the Lotus Sutra and who reached Nirvana at the end of their journey, can't reach the level of Atma or God, so they do not comment on God. *Sun-Moon-Brigh*t is mentioned in Lotus Sutra as one of the sons of the Creation.

Even Lotus Sutra mentions that Gautam Buddha was not the actual original Buddha, but he was the 16th son of Buddha. *This is mentioned in Chapter- Phantom City, where it is mentioned that the top level Buddha had 16 sons,* and Gautam Buddha was the youngest. So History of the Lotus Sutra tells that Lotus Sutra was followed by one bright star, and to spread the message of Lotus Sutra further, Buddha Sentients were introduced from the source of Lotus Sutra. Afterward, many Buddhas came on this Path. ***They all went to Nirvana in the ultimate Buddha, which is Emptiness. Each Buddha handed over the baton of the Lotus Sutra to the next Buddha.***

Assuming all of this, there should be no conflict; Hinduism, Vedas, and Buddhism are the same. Buddhism is the continuation of the Vedas, and it is a product of Emptiness. I can say that another word for Emptiness is Maya which is used in Vedas If we analyse all these factors, and go deep into it, we will find that there is uniformity in Hinduism, Christianity, Islam or Sikhism- they are all part of the Lotus Sutra.

Out of this Maya or Emptiness, Buddhas are formed only after a live entity comes in contact with Lotus Sutra and starts rising. Lotus Sutra is the only Vehicle in which they can rise, and they can become Bodhisattvas[25].

So there are many levels of Bodhisattvas, a lower level, a higher Bodhisattva, etc.; each Bodhisattva has grown on the principle of some quality of Lotus Sutra.

Jesus Christ had a quality of Compassion. Compassion means he could take the pain and suffering of others in his body to an unlimited extent. That is how he got connected to Lotus Sutra and rose to some extent to be the Son of God.

In the same way, I think the Koran mentions Emptiness as the highest level of God. That means no photo or form of Allah. It is sort of Unseen, Adrishya God. Prophet Mohammad is a product of Allah.

If we understand there is only one God. and everything came out of him, then we have to understand everything logically and that is how I have made some decisions in my mind.

I treat Hindus, Muslims, Christians, Sikhs, and others as brothers and sisters, as part of the creation, almost the same as me. The religion that divides us because of the control of Prophets or Powers of religious heads / Gurus is only to a limited extent.

---

25 Courtesy (ref Pg 33 of LS book)

When we rise and go higher, things go on uniting and ultimately reaching an Atma level which is a subdivision of God. God can withdraw everyone back into Himself to a higher awareness.

Summary Of Gyaan For Self Benefit

I want to live peacefully, and that peacefulness will come only when my body's needs are fulfilled and there is no physical or mental pain. I should not feel even the fear of Death. For this, a summary has been made so that everyone can benefit from it. There are three things that we have to take care of:

First is **Ego.** Our ego causes lots of problems, and it has no existence. But this ego, when it confronts *awareness* in you, the ego disappears, and the awareness comes into the picture. Awareness is the nature of God. So you can assume that when you are aware, everything is managed by God and not by your Ego and you have to remember that this is a very important step.

The second step is **Wisdom**: Ignorance has to be abolished by the wisdom of Lotus Sutra. God's awareness is very much required to fulfill our ambition. The process is through many layers where its nature is ignorance. So in order, the God should have availability of gyaan over ignorance, one's mind should be attached to the Lotus Sutra or should be in contact with the Lotus Sutra. This is very important. *This is also a challenging thing. So if one cannot connect directly to Lotus Sutra, then one should connect with a* *person who is in connection with Lotus Sutra. The purpose will be served. The only thing is that your difficulties and sufferings are now exchanged with the person connected with Lotus Sutra, who dissolves your Karmas.* It is a barter system, give and take. In a sense, with the benefit it gives you, you have to give back the services to it. This can be done through our creation; Our creation is our body and mind.

The third step is **Creation.** Your body's creation is your own; it indicates mistakes that your creation has made by your emotions and feelings of suffering pain and negative emotions like fear of death. Body and mind are indicators. When the Body is suffering, it indicates something is wrong. Wrong can be due to *Intakes or Ignorance.* We take the air, water, and food as intakes, and mentally we take emotions from our surroundings. If you are busy creating something helpful to others, then Karma will give back the facility of comfort and luxury. If we surrender all these things to the person linked to Lotus Sutra or Lotus Sutra itself, it can take care of the defects, and your body will be perfect.

Now I will also give details. This gyaan (knowledge) is not meant for ordinary people. This is meant for those who want deep contact with Lotus Sutra. The difficulty in direct contact with the Lotus Sutra is that there is a required gate from which one has to enter the **Lotus Sutra, and the Gate is Emptiness.** Emptiness can be achieved by awareness of your body.

The level of emptiness can be low or high. If you are at a low level of emptiness, you can grow beyond that level, as again there will be intake and you can again achieve emptiness repeatedly. Ultimately you will reach a state of awareness where your door of emptiness opens, and you can directly reach the Lotus Sutra. Lotus Sutra is similar to a computer that has taken all the information of all the life that has been created in billions of years, sorted it out, and extracted wisdom. Hence, contact with Lotus Sutra helps clear all the mistakes our body makes out of ignorance. So a person who is in direct contact with the Lotus Sutra will have that benefit. Company with the Saint, the Master of Lotus Sutra, will give you the facility to neutralize any negative mistakes that happened out of ignorance that cause you to suffer.

If one wants to go into details of how this Lotus Sutra works, there is also a sort of Indication. Our body has Seven Chakras. Seven chakras is the path mentioned in Hinduism for attaining Moksh- freedom from repeated cycles of Birth and death and also freedom from pain and suffering, but that, unfortunately, leaves all the elements of your body behind. You, as a Self or Ego, get destroyed, nothing happens. *Ego from someone else takes over those elements, and the name gets changed.* So these Seven Chakras are a mirage that Lotus Sutra tells in the first chapter itself. If you are in contact with Lotus Sutra, it subsequently creates three bodies around you, i.e., *Sambhog Kaya, Nirmaan Kaya & Dharam Kaya.* If you want Lotus Sutra to work efficiently for you, then you have to spend time creating, that adds to your creation and adds to your *Nirman Kaaya.*

The second thing is that your creation should be helpful for a very long time in many lives and to many people. The more it is helpful to more lives or people, the more benefit it will give you. So for that, Dharma Kaya is required. The benefit of wise creation, which benefits others, accumulates in your *Sambhog Kaya.* Sambhog Kaya is a sort of bank account which you have made for others and others who have benefited from your creation and have to pay back by giving service to you so that your existence becomes easy.

Prosperity & Abundance

As soon as I started meditation in 1992, I remember receiving one fascinating message from an ant. One day, I was on the porch and saw an ant moving around. It found a cluster of food that would be enough for many ants. The ant tried moving it but couldn't, so it started dancing around it. I was surprised to see this action of the ant, but after a while, I noticed a colony of ants coming toward it. Earlier, there were no ants around, and now I saw a colony!!! Where did they appear from? I was surprised. The colony of ants took the cluster of food and left.

When I sat in meditation, I got a message saying I would understand a lot when I studied more about ants & bees.

The studies in scientific papers revealed[26] that ants are a fascinating bunch of creatures capable of a great many things. They have complex social structures. Ant colonies are biologically programmed to have strict roles for each member of their colony. That structure is vital to their survival. This complex system divides nests into three roles: queen, breeders, and workers. After breeding, the Queen ant sheds its wings and begins digging for its new nest.

Breeders are all males and are also all born with wings. They will fly off to breed with new queen ants. Once they have finished that breeding cycle, Ant males die. Worker ants are all females, separated into soldiers,

26(Courtesy)https://bluebeetlepest.com/general-pests/what-happens-when-an-ant-queen-dies/

excavators, foragers, garbage collectors, and gardeners. Each ant's role is defined by its size, and the diet they feed on is larvae.

I still could not figure out how one ant had communicated with others to come and collect food despite being so far from others. I discovered that only the queen ant could communicate with all the other ants, just like Wifi, whereas other ants can only communicate a message to the queen ant. Ants communicate with each other through chemicals called pheromones. When I understood their system, I wondered why humans do not have similar systems built in. It would benefit the human race in a big way.

Further studies revealed that one colony of ants stayed away from another colony. Sometimes different colonies of ants fight and even kill each other. Red ants are fighters, but black ants are peaceful. When the Queen ant's life is nearing an end, another ant starts growing and develops wings. Soon after queen ant dies, a new one takes its place. The dead Queen ant is given a proper burial. If a Queen ant dies unexpectedly, the whole colony of ants slowly falls apart as the colony can no longer reproduce, leaving the colony doomed and it dies off completely.

During my meditation, I receive messages. I feel there must be quite a few who receive these messages, but most of us are deprived of them. Imagine if all of us earthlings were tuned to this energy; we all would be in a much better place. But this doesn't seem possible unless all of us become meditators and understand Lotus Sutra.

Even if a select few could develop this WiFi communication system, we can make this world a beautiful place to live in. It is known that when the Universe came into being, such a communication system existed between Gods. With good intentions and proper understanding of the Oneness of the Universe, this Wifi communication system could bring Nations together. One policy would exist, there would be no need for a visa or even passports, and life would be so much of a superior quality.

I am looking forward to such a Universe.

Even the place in which we reside has a story behind it. I was 80 years old, too sick and felt as good as dead. However, I revived one day and stopped medication. So the thought arose in me that I had stopped all medicines, and now it is up to me to regain good health. I had one cousin in Dubai who had written that he would love to settle in Pune, and wanted me to suggest some good places for him in Pune.

I started looking around near my locality. I remembered that my son, Sunil, had taken me to a Golf area some 8-10 years back in Neeco Park. That site would be a good place for him to reside, so I suggested it to my cousin.

When he came to know about it, he came there and bought a flat and took another flat on rent so that he could stay there till the papers of the flat he had bought were handed over to him. He invited me to his rented flat. I liked it a lot and got the idea that I could take a one-bedroom apartment and enjoy the open air, go swimming in the posh society, and play golf to recover my lost health.

I wanted it for rent, so I talked it over to my cousin. I located a flat within the society, talked to its owner, and discussed the terms of rent for 11 months on lease. I finally rented it. My family found it very strange that I had taken an apartment on lease when we had a comfortable bungalow to reside in for so many years, but they consented. I was determined to regain my health.

I started going there daily for 2-3 hours. Sunil finally came along with his children to see the activities I did there, and they and my grandson started regularly visiting for swimming and playing golf. About 3 - 4 months passed, and my health gradually improved. In between, I bought a Golf set to play in the Golf area provided inside the Society and started Walking, Swimming and improving my health.

After 5- 6 months, I asked Sunil whether we could buy a good apartment here as my lease for 11 months will end in a few months. He said he, too, was thinking of buying a 5-6 bedroom apartment. But the budget was too high for him. It took him another 2 - 3 months. Sunil was perplexed and could not decide. In the same posh society, while playing golf regularly at the end of the section where the high-rise Apartments row ended, the section of the Villa started, which I used to observe.

Again while playing Golf, one day, *I envisioned myself standing on the rooftop of the last villa at the end of the row.* We were not even thinking of buying a flat, and my dream of a high-end villa, which was way out of our league, made me ridicule my high hopes.

So Villa # 56 came to be ours at the end of the row of villas. How? Let us see. Its price was way too high initially, and it was just an empty framework inside. Then rates started decreasing, and my lease ended, so Sunil told me to extend the lease until we decided. One day while we were swimming in the Society club he asked me which flat I liked here. I said I liked the Villa at the end. Sunil laughed, saying it was already taken up and its price was beyond our capacity. I laughed over it because I knew it was going to be ours. How? I do not know.

In Meditation, first, we go through Hell with all the negative Spirits giving us sickness and ill health, and after having gone through that phase, we rise where Devis and Devtas from Heaven come to take us. They spoil us so much that we can lose our balance.

One day while in Meditation, I saw that I was standing on the balcony of Villa no. 56 and the golf course was full of people who had come from all over the world to take my blessings. The location and Villa in vision was quite central by road and air as there was a helipad in the complex. I liked what I saw as I played golf here and my health had improved. My son, Sunil's health, was not good either and I felt his health and quality of life would improve considerably if we had property here. I could visualize my children and grandchildren playing golf with enthusiasm. But *Sunil was looking for an apartment, and we had no plan of buying a villa.* It was beyond our budget too. After enquiring, Sunil came to know it was already bought.

Unexpectedly, circumstances turned around in our favor. The price fell, and the Villa became vacant. All at once, one of Sunil's properties also got sold, and he had cash in hand. It surprisingly looked like we could afford the Villa after all. There was strong opposition when the proposal was put forward to the family. *Surprisingly all obstacles cleared by themselves, and we finally had possession of the Villa in hand.*

The Vision to buy the Villa was seen only when I was connected to Lotus Sutra meditation and I consider it as HIS blessing. My life has become magical because of the presence of the Lotus Sutra in my life. My way of viewing things has completely changed, and I have gained a lot of mastery over things I never even knew. I'm experiencing a lot of miraculous powers in my life because of the presence of the Lotus Sutra.

Jhanas

For the last 30 years, I have been meditating. Earlier I used to absorb all the negativity and ill health of people around me. As a result, my health started to deteriorate, and there came the point when my body could take it no more. I was going to die. I felt I could not walk this Path anymore. Gautam Buddha mentions these health problems as ***Jhanas*[27] *(Wisdom body, anti-virus system).*** I died but then came back to my body in 2017, when I was 80 years old. The message I got was that it was not my time yet. I still had a lot of work to do. *"You have to go back to Earth, my son. Although your body is in bad shape as you have done a lot of work, you will recover. Do as much as you can now".*

I refer to this Antivirus System as Jhana. During my 30 years of meditation, I have physically experienced this and the best term I find for this is Jhana which has been used in many Buddha books written in Pali language, but not referred much in Lotus Sutra by Burton Watson.

So despite doctors telling me that I did not have much time to live and they informing my son about my poor health condition, I threw away all medicines I was taking and I recovered slowly.

---

27 The Jhanas in Theravada Buddist Meditation (ref Appendix pg xlii)

(Courtesy :

https://www.accesstoinsight.org/lib/authors/gunaratana/wheel351.html#:~:text=twofol d%20meaning%20of,of%20the%20fruits.)

Now I soak only in knowledge and avoid all negativity. My body has learned the hard way.

I do not know if this impacts my surroundings, but I see improvement everywhere. I know my daily life has everything in abundance. In my family, I have abundant wealth with all comforts and luxuries. Even the locality where I live has improved. The world is getting to be a better place. I believe meditation has the power to improve lives to a higher level. I see things at different levels improving. I have come to know the purpose of my life.

But now, by the age of 85 years, I have limited my area of attack in this Era. I fought the same war a billion and trillion years ago, and at a particular time, I must have left this war because the Earth could not be free from Old age, Death & Suffering. I have continued the same war in this life and moved it further to greater heights.

In the Vedas, we see mention of many Avatars. Let us observe the Fish. The struggle must have been arduous when Fish attempted to change to a tortoise and walk on land. The fish must have been determined to move to land; just like in Lotus Sutra, *Sun-Moon-Bright* (in the chapters of Lotus Sutra, it is mentioned) attempted to survive longer. The seed of determination had been sown in the Fish. Thus in a constant attempt to go on to land, it died several times and was reborn again. That determination made it successful. When meteorites rained on top of it, it adapted to the changes over many lifetimes and gradually transformed by *building a hard shell on top* of it to become a tortoise. It gave birth to many children, and gradually, they ruled the Earth.

My struggles are similar in attempting to become a Buddha in the stage of Emptiness. In between these struggles, my daughter was usurped by ghosts. The ghosts made me so passive that I was not conscious of myself. I was sick and had a fall which broke my back. This was in 2005-2006 after my daughter died. I was as good as dead. This did not make me sad but angry with God and myself, as my daughter had gone. Soon even I would die with all my sickness.

I was furious and upset with myself. *What had I done to get such a severe punishment? Gita had gone and I, too, was on my deathbed.*

Like a fish out of water, I was angry and determined to fight. I had wronged no one, nor had I harmed anyone. This should not have happened to me. Since the passion to walk free on this path was strong, Divinity helped me. My story didn't end here.

Night after night, I took the dangerous journey to Hell in search of my daughter Gita. Many ferocious ghosts interfered with my Astral travel. I used to come back in my body drained and then meditate and make myself all right. On some days I used to be so wounded that it would take 3 - 4 days to recover from the pain. But I was desperate to reach my daughter.

I remember in Mahabharat, Arjuna's son Abhimanyu was killed when the army of Duryodhan surrounded him by building a wall in between him & Pandavas, who were entering with him.

I, too, had a ferocious fight with many ghosts and Spirits who had taken my daughter away deep within their circle. Every night for more than ten years, I suffered. I was becoming weak. Every time I entered the Hell, I met many ghosts and Spirits, some of whom I cleansed and sent purified to Heaven. Out of their habit, they used to push their nature on me, wound me and stab me. I grew weak and immensely sick. I tried to make them understand, but they were unaffected. I had not found my daughter yet.

By the age of 80 years, and it was eleven years since my daughter had passed away, I had all the health problems. I had a weak heart; my gallbladder was painful; I had urine trouble; my eyes, ears, and teeth all had weakened. Nothing was right with me.

Although I was in excruciating pain and doctors gave up hope, the only thing that kept me going was my determination to find my daughter. That night I cried, complaining to God, *"As long as Lotus Sutra is with me, I cannot die without being in a state of awareness. How am I to leave my body if I endure immense pain? How will I remember to continue the struggle to reach my daughter in my next life?"*. God then gave me a shield of protection from ghosts and Spirits , of which I have mentioned earlier. Feeling safe now, I treaded the lokas of ghosts and Spirits two-three times a day with caution. I entered their world and purified many such Spirits over the years. Although I went deep many times during the day, I still could not reach Gitu.

30th June 2022 was the day I was told I would be rewarded for my relentless effort. This was after the death of the evil Master who was responsible for the demise of my daughter Gitu.

She was unconscious, shriveled, wounded, scarred, and in immense pain. I could see her sleeping. Her whole body was immensely wounded. My eyes were tearful. I hugged her. I treated her with my spiritual powers. I picked up her wounded body and got her back on my Plane. I also cleansed the Spirits who had wounded her and sent them back.

"Gitu, nobody can take over you now. The ghosts and Spirits will never harm you. I will make you as clean as before. You will be well as before and free to walk wherever you want".

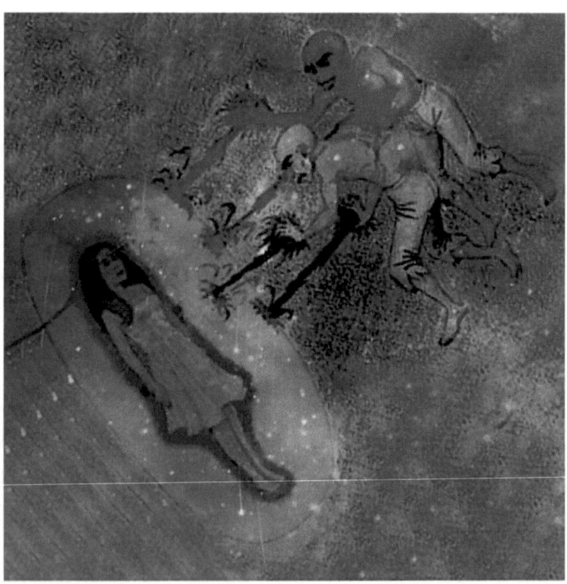

I do not regret helping the ghost and Spirits because they were following their nature of stabbing and poaching. That was their basic nature. Their fate was to eat away other Souls. I used to enter their world and cleanse them. In doing so, I received their powers. Their powers would decrease, and mine would increase. Of course, I suffered a lot in the process. But that was my dharma.

The three experiences of my Inner Voice/ Guidance and controlled mind-talk that had a significant impact on my life were:

Initially, the Soul of a good Spirit resided in me. It gave answers to all my questions through the inner voice, Guru. It was like a small voice of a Spirit that nudged my hearing aid with answers.

The second was the ghastly Spirit which controlled my body. That Spirit had utterly taken over my Body. Its only purpose was to occupy my body and totally possess me. But through the awareness meditation, that powerful Spirit was gradually dissolved. I calmed it down by sending it a lot of positive energy and it left for its abode feeling light. Through this Spirit, I realized my capabilities as a spiritual medium and tried to channel myself for my spiritual journey ahead.

I had the third and the most dangerous impact after the death of my loving daughter Gitu. I had reached the stage of death after having a nasty fall. My spine had broken. The Spirit which came to possess me at that time was the Phantom, the King of Ghost. There were many Spirits under his control. It might be possible that the Master I met earlier had a deep connection with these demonic Spirits. He was like ruling party anarchy, a very powerful Master. He might have captured/seized my mind, and I felt like a Zombie.

In the struggle that ensued within, my back healed gradually.

My Guru's wisdom resounded in my ears, *"The whole world is within you. We are all ONE. Due to ignorance, the spirits have reached this Plane. Fear and ignorance is in their nature and they use their powers. Their negative energy slows our Universe from progressing further. You exist in a different plane. Your power wants this Universe to progress, be happy, free of suffering and health issues".*

A battle of ideas ensued. The Spirits wanted to expand their kingdom and make it vast by thrusting their ideas. The Demon Master I met in physical form in the Ashram was doing the same. He wanted to control others. The fight lasted for 15 years, from the time I met him in 1995 till 2005 when my daughter died.

I wanted to help these Spirits because my daughter Gita had been annexed by these Spirits of the Demon Master and could not have been happy. I had to give her freedom. My Guru's purpose was to get this Universe to progress and make it a happy place by removing negativity from people that surrounded the mindset of many. *To weaken their mindset, I used to take in their negativity, convert it into positive and release them.*

My powers and I were united. Every night I slept and when I was unaware, the ghosts entered my body. The pain, struggle and negativity that entered would sometimes be unbearable and I would be wide awake. Every night from around 3 am onwards; I would sit with awareness and meditate for long hours till I felt the pain subside. I was actually doing a type of Shraadh, a pind-daan for all lost souls. *It is believed that Pitra Paksha rites, liberate a soul from the vicious circle of life and death and helps it in attaining salvation. Similarly, I use to release these lost souls, from the clutches of Hell, to go on with their next birth. Was Gitu's death a part of my learning process,Yes, O! But why is spiritual realization such a painful process?*

The difference between the departed mortals and the mortals of this plane is that the mortals of this plane are clothed with the garment of flesh, bone, and blood, while the departed souls are clothed with a finer substance of thought and feelings. They can penetrate through a wall, but human beings need a door, and that is the only difference between us and departed souls. They are just as much within the realm of death as we are. Death means a change of our physical garment. It is wrong to think that death means total destruction or absolute annihilation. The wise know that when the transformation of our life takes place, our life reverts to its elementary condition. This means a coming and going. It is the realm of birth and rebirth.

My family wanted to know why Gitu had to suffer so much. The fact is, Gitu had accumulated some Karmas before she was born as my daughter. As a result, a hostile entity overpowered her mind and took her to an unknown place of suffering and helplessness. The nature of these entities is to survive on the Cosmic Energy of the human who still has the zest for life. Gitus' ignorance about them made it possible for them. The negative Karma of the entity that took her away started now. Gitu, on the contrary, accumulated Karmas of suffering, which she would be paid back positively in one of her lives. The entities' Karmas equaled the suffering Gitu went through. The Master who got these entities also made Karma. These entities kept sucking the energy out of her till she had life.

I chased these entities to help Gitu. Even if I had not chased them, these entities have a limit, and they break down by themselves after a while. When they did break, Gitu became free from Karmas and recovery started. The same entities have to pay her back. But we do not know when that will happen. In her case, I reached out to her.

I blamed myself for her suffering because I had met the Demon Master first and through him, her suffering started. I was linked with her Karma. To pay her back, I put in all my effort to track her. I had decided to clear my Karma and drive those negative energies away, that the entity had put on her. When I found her, I pulled their ears and made them beg for forgiveness from Gitu. Gitu has recovered quickly and these ghosts can not trouble her any more as they are under my control now. They have not dispersed. This is, in fact, their path. They are lucky because they have a path to clear their Karma because of me.

Gitu's negative Karmas changed to positive, and she will become better than before as she has gained wisdom about how entities attack despite her no involvement and how that leads to suffering. There are multiple options for her to move on. She will either gain knowledge about them on how to be safe from its pitfalls or hold the hands of a Guru who can take care of her. All Gurus have a limit. Heaven has 16 levels. Some Gurus are of a high level, and some are at other low levels. It depends on her luck whose hand she holds. Holding the hands of a high-level Guru will give her complete protection, whereas lower-level Gurus have limitations. They take you as far as they can and then release you. But where do you get knowledge of such Gurus?

This knowledge shows us what is right and wrong. This understanding changes with each situation. Lotus Sutra is the only one that tells us that souls when they enter emptiness, store their wisdom in the form of Jhanas. Scores of Souls' Understanding are stored in the Lotus Sutra. Lotus Sutra is also a Guru, and the one who understands it and holds its hand will face the situations successfully with guidance from Lotus Sutra. Your life becomes smooth as Lotus Sutra takes you to the highest level. This is the right path. If a Soul goes through suffering and comes out of it in a few years, such a Soul is considered very lucky as they came out in a short time as some Souls suffer for many lifetimes.

This is not important. The important thing here is how much have they understood about the right and wrong things in their life and how much wisdom and creativity were they able to apply to themselves. Otherwise, punishment for bad karma and pleasure for right does come. The level is fixed, and life goes on. Suppose you do not finish your Karma even after thousands of lifetimes; you will go into Moksh. You become a tiny insect and disappear and then go back to your Guru's energy. No one goes out. Everyone goes to their Source taking some or the other path. There are two Sources. One is God, and the other is Emptiness.

Emptiness is a Shadow of God. Or it is God's Maya or its mirror image. Emptiness is addressed by many names. It has the same properties as God because it is a mirror image. God divides himself into several parts and descends down and, again, with awareness, pulls everything up. But Emptiness is also like God. When it divides itself and comes down, it does not have the power to go back up in the Universe. We all have a significant part of that Emptiness in us. Our bodies, our senses, and our minds all are made of Emptiness. We are a part of Emptiness. We are Creation. Only a tiny part of the awareness of God is in us.

Some saints catch hold of God's Hands and go to Moksh. Leaving our creation, we can go to Guru, or someone can hold us. If you consider yourself as a part of creation, then to change creation in a better way, you need wisdom which is Lotus Sutra.

Either you follow the path of wisdom of Lotus Sutra and become a huge creation to be born as a king. The capacity to become king of planets comes in you. *Merging with God does not make sense when you are in the low category of wisdom.* Do whatever you want because the path of creation can be treated only with wisdom with the guidance of the Lotus Sutra.

If you have no interest in creation, then go back to God. *We must remember that God himself had come down to create the Universe, and your soul came down as creation to do your duty that God wishes, but you ignore his wish and want to go back, without fulfilling God's objective. Then God sent someone else, a part of himself, down. It means you came and went back with no achievement. When in fact, the one who creates creation as per God's wish gets placed to a much higher level, we call them Bodhisattvas.*

Contemplation of The Book Of Lotus Sutra

The painting gives the idea of the Lotus Sutra. Meditation is not isolating. It first isolates and collects cosmic energy and then distributes it to society.

I refer to Lotus Sutra, translated by Burton Watson. I have understood 60% of the Lotus Sutra in my 36 years of meditation. Reading each line and practically applying it has brought a lot of change in me. I am now posting and discussing some pages which explain Lotus Sutra, so that you get tuned to the way Lotus Sutra works.

Lotus Sutra Book...Translated by Burton Watson[28]

28 Lotus Sutra Book...Translated by Burton Watson

Courtesy:

(https://ia802902.us.archive.org/13/items/lotussutraburtonwatson_202003_473_o/Lotus%20Sutra%20Burton%20Watson.pdf)

All Buddhas, Past, Present And Future Abide In Emptiness And Follow The Path Of One Vehicle.[29]

- **Pg 14 of Lotus Sutra**[30] discusses *Sun-Moon-Bright* Buddha, who started the birth of Lotus Sutra. He is the one who had to die 20,000 times. In each Era, the *Sun-Moon-Bright* Buddha appeared and followed a Path, and when the Era ended, all these disappeared. This happened 20,000 times. This was the process of his understanding of how to survive in existence. There were many millions of *Sun-Moons* in the sky, and in each Era, they appeared and disappeared. **One *Sun-Moon-Bright* Buddha was trying to survive the era and become the**

29 (ref pg 33 of LS book)

30 (ref pg 14 of LS book)

biggest star of the era so that he could defeat evolution and survive and be the Best Star of The Universe. This he could do by understanding the emptiness of the system.

When one understands emptiness, one doesn't demand light from other Suns or give any light to others. It just stands silently, peacefully in emptiness. If some nearby star or Sun comes and takes away its light, he allows it, or if it comes and bombards it with its light, he accepts it. This is the method by which the first wisdom of Lotus Sutra started.

A time came when this *Sun-Moon-Bright* did not disappear at the end of the Era. It remained and later on, in the next Era, he started his journey, which was better than any other *Sun-Moon-Bright*. This gave him confidence that he had learned the method of survival in this era. Lotus Sutra, in fact, tells about it, that anybody who survives at the end of the era is called *Bodhisattva*. One who has done things that the creation wants. When the creation is advanced, they survive. All other things that do not advance the creation fade away. It is a formation of *Sambhog Kaaya with the help of Nirman and Dharma Kaaya*. This Sambhog Kaaya does not disappear at the end of the era, and that portion survives the era for the next era to come.

- **This page also talks about (last three lines of Pg14)** the birth of eight princely sons to this Buddha. Evolution has to move on. These eight sons were all connected to the mind of Buddha, and whenever the voice of Buddha reached their minds, they would follow it. In Fact, they were an extended part of *Sun-Moon-Bright* Buddha. When any Buddha goes to Nirvana, his sons continue with the work of the father, and that way, the Lotus Sutra extends its horizon to reach and preach to the masses so that they could take advantage of this divine knowledge.

In the life of Bees and Ants, when the Queen dies, another worker rises to take the place of this Queen by developing wings and growing in size so that it can continue the reign of the earlier Queen.Thus the whole colony survives. So it is an extension of the life period of Buddha or his sons continuing with their work.

For e.g. every day I am gathering cosmic energy and expanding my body. Initially, it satisfied my desires, and those desires were meant for my body, my family, and my neighbors, but then the flow of energy still goes on continuing and increasing, and this energy then works for surroundings, cities, and later on, surrounding countries. Along with that, my method is to extend the life period by certain years. Then I should be capable of creating sons through this Cosmic energy who would be totally connected to me, and they can carry this work like Queen Bee Ant's work can continue to the next generation.

- **<u>Pg 134</u>**[31] tells about Gautam Buddha's previous lives. Millions of years ago, he was the 16th son of Buddha. Shakyamuni Buddha is a name given to him who lived from 566 BC to 485BC in central India. So the basic Lotus Sutra is a collection of wisdom from many, many years.

The message in all is that *"There is only One Vehicle."* There are no other vehicles that are known. That Vehicle is EMPTINESS. A rain shower comes down on those connected to Lotus Sutra. The intensity of the shower varies depending on each individual's connection with the Lotus Sutra.

Maitryaniputra Purna, a perfect Bodhisattva, was a very advanced Bodhisattva who understood Lotus Sutra in many ways. He could utilize the benefits of Lotus Sutra for others as well. Initially, when I read this book. I thought probably I am Purna, who has taken rebirth in this world because I am the only person who has been using Lotus Sutra not only for the benefit of my body, not only for the benefit of my family but also for the World as a whole.

We human beings, when we get associated or connected with Lotus Sutra; our connection may be weak or may be strong as well; depending on the strength of the connection, we pass on our negative energies into the cosmic energy of the Lotus Sutra. *The Lotus Sutra then filters it back to us in pure form, and, when*

---

31 (refer pg 134 of LS book)

that pure energy comes back to our body, that is an additional life source for us. This benefit is not available to those not connected to Lotus Sutra.

This knowledge is perfectly known to me and also to Purna. Suppose I accumulate this pure energy continuously and go on storing it in my body, in the form of Dharma Kaaya, Nirmaan Kaaya, or Sambhog Kaaya. I can then ascend from the existing plane to the higher plane, which is also the quality of the Lotus Sutra. That's why it is called only ONE VEHICLE, which can take you up, which can lift you. Lotus Sutra is the ONLY VEHICLE that can take you back to your Source from where you came down. There are many other benefits that Bodhisattvas normally know. For e.g. a simple Bodhisattva will know that if I speak truth, I am always getting connected to some portion of the Lotus Sutra. He only knows that truth is something good. A small Bodhisattva understands that if he gets his parents and children to grow nicely in a nice and correct way, he will ascend. So these are different categories of Bodhisattvas; Purna is an example of an exemplary Bodhisattva who has reached a higher state of understanding.

Purna Maitryani Putra was a disciple of Gautam Buddha and a very ordinary person in the whole gathering. There were many disciples of Gautam Buddha who were famous and above Purna. They established and controlled huge ashrams and were given importance by Buddha. But this Purna was unknown to anyone except Gautam Buddha, who also knew his past and Purna's achievements. Probably this indicates that a very highly advanced Bodhisattva need not appear as a big personality. He could be a very ordinary person in society doing good work in the background. But the work goes on, on a very extensive scale through him. He has no desire to publicize his work at all. For example, I want to see whether my way is working. I wanted to see it, and there was no other method except to compare the prosperity around me. On the other hand, Purna did not have any desire or expect any appreciation from others and continued with his good work, having full faith in himself. Gautam Budha talked about him in a gathering and said that he was one of his hidden gems.

- Lotus Sutra has a couple of Chapters in which a point has been explained by giving stories: ***Simile and Parable, Pg 68***[32] refers to Lotus Sutra to a person who was in connection with any Buddha in previous Era/ birth and by default with Lotus Sutra also. So he has given an example:

  That Lotus Sutra is like a gem tied to one's clothes and in the next birth though he forgets Lotus Sutra, the gem which is tied to his cloth reminds/ helps him to go beyond the miseries and gain back the connection.

  I like this Parable because I remember I was born in a family which always talked about Guru Nanak,

32 Courtesy: refer pg 68 of LS book

Shiva, or other deities or God. Somebody talked about Gautam Buddha also, but it was just a name for me, and Lotus Sutra was the word that most of us had never heard.

It is the gem that was probably tied to me in my previous birth to my body. This gem reminded me of Lotus Sutra in this birth, and this has been a constant source of inspiration for me because I say an ignorant person like me born in this birth could revive Lotus Sutra from my previous births. That means even in future births; I will follow the Lotus Sutra. I will continue growing in Lotus Sutra; this is the inspiration I got and I feel so good about this.

Kalki is one of the Sons of God. He lives in the upper planes 0 to 15 and comes down to lower levels to extend the creation. Presently he has come down to Earth plane i.e.26th plane along with the Lotus Sutra of Buddha system.

- In *Ch 15, Burton Watson's – Lotus Sutra* ***'Emerging from Earth'.*** If you read this Chapter, it describes the coming down of Buddha some billions years ago in the previous Era and doing the work along with *Kalki of that Yuga to* clean the creation. It is not mentioned specifically as Kalki, but as Bodhisattvas working all together to clean the Universe. It is for us to use our wisdom to understand this. At the end of every Kalpa after killing Evilness, his life span increases, he takes re-birth, with much better creativity and wisdom.

Some trillion-billion years earlier, this Avatar had developed the Buddha System along with Lotus Sutra. Initially he had to take birth 20,000 times before the concept of Lotus Sutra developed in His mind.

Since then He has been coming down in the form of Kalki Avatar and working from Plane 16 toward Plane 31. Now He is working through me (Ram Peswani) at Plane no. 26 and I had taken birth here, many times in previous Eras. Each time I came, the system of cleaning in Plane no. 26 advanced further and the time has now come to continue that work. Plane no. 16 required my birth 20,000 times. This present Plane no. 26- Earth may require my birth only a few times. His (Kalki's) purpose is to free the Existence from suffering, old age and death.

- **<u>Pg 63 of Lotus Sutra</u> describes the Suffering[33] in detail.**

  I do not come down to the Planes, till life is ready to receive the Lotus Sutra from the Buddha System. So coming down to Earth in each Era. i.e Plane 26 depends upon the coming down of Buddha first and after Buddha comes and hands over the Lotus Sutra to some appropriate persons who can keep it alive in their body. In this Era some 2050 years back, the person was Gautam Buddha who was the

---

33 (ref Pg 63 of LS book)

16th son of earlier Buddha i.e. described in chapter 7 Phantom City[34].

- **On page 134 of Lotus Sutra,** it has been mentioned that He had come down to 26th Plane and handed over the Lotus Sutra to many of his devotees. In this book of Lotus Sutra, pg 134, mentions Shakyamuni, was the 16th son of the historical Buddha of the previous Era.

In every Era the System of ten Avatars is followed on Earth in the 26th Plane whereas in Plane no.16, when only one Avatar was required. Only *Sun-Moon-Bright* was required because life did not have many details and forms. By the time, life on Earth evolved, a human being had formed through the process of Avatars and I am now the Tenth Avatar in Plane no. 26.

Before I come down to Earth I have a lot of preparations to do. As I described, first, I have to wait till first Buddha descends and hands Lotus Sutra to many suitable persons[35].

- You can see this in CH 1, pgs 3 to 6 of the LOTUS SUTRA. In the CH 1, Buddha gives his ultimate teaching to those worthy of it. On pg 15[36], 3rd Para

---

34Courtesy : Gautham Buddha was also known as Shakyamuni Buddha who was 16th son of historical Buddha. (refer pg 134 of LS book)

35 Courtesy : refer pgs 3 to 6 of Lotus Sutra book

36 Courtesy : refer pg 15 of Lotus Sutra book

4th line says: *...When he finished preaching the Sutra...*

Buddha came to the mountain Girdhar Kutti at Rajgad in Bihar and he handed over the Lotus Sutra to many of his disciples.[37]

It was very important for Gautam Buddha that this Lotus Sutra should be preserved. Though he knew that it was very difficult for a normal person to understand, a devotee who has blind faith in him (Gautam Buddha), will do as Gautam Buddha tells him. So He said that this Lotus Sutra should be recited in all Mahanaya temples. *It takes about three hours to complete and every disciple of His should do this full Sutra with devotion so that it is preserved for Kalki to come and receive it. The importance of the Lotus Sutra can be understood from the fact that Kalki is nothing if he doesn't have this Lotus Sutra, which is the Sword of Wisdom.* So since the last 2560 years, in thousands and thousands of Mahayana temples in various parts of the globe, many disciples gather everyday after lunch and recite this whole Lotus Sutra along with drums, chanting and singing so that this Sutra is preserved. After the death of Gautam Buddha some 500 years later, writing was devised. It was decided that the Lotus Sutra should be preserved in a prime location in every temple and should be written in Golden Ink and its cover should also be gold so that people understand the extreme importance of

---

37 Courtesy : refer pg 3 of Lotus Sutra book

preserving this Lotus Sutra and respect and worship it. They thought that the best way to preserve the Lotus Sutra was by worshiping and reciting the same by the devotees, even though they did not understand fully or recite the lines in it in poem form. So Gautam Buddha who started this System 2560 years back had brought down this Lotus Sutra from *Phantom City* and left this System on Earth and Lotus Sutra has been kept alive as per the instructions of Lotus Sutra even now. Again I iterate for the readers to read *The Lotus Sutra* Book by Burton Watson or click on the link mentioned in the *ebook* for the mentioned pages of that Book.

The time had come for Kalki now to search for a suitable person on Earth in this Twenty-first century who as a devotee has preserved this Lotus Sutra in his body and that Sutra can again grow back to become a Weapon for Kalki for Cleaning this Earth. So this was a very important point for the Kalki to search for such a suitable person and with his extraordinary clearness, he found me (Ram Peswani) at the age of about 15 years in 1951. I was sleeping on a cot outside Dev Nagar home and looking at the sky. The Star identified me, got connected to me and decided to reside in my body.

Heaven, Hell, Rebirth, And Karma

If all Karmas are cleared by going to Hell and Heaven, why are we Reborn?

There was God and God alone, and He wanted to create, so he divided himself from one entity into many, up to 31 planes. By the time God's division reached the 31st plane, it was in microsize. When God started division, the first plane was a **macro** or a huge creation with high awareness and power. At the micro level, the awareness and power were bare minimum and almost negligible. God also had communication barriers due to this. The splitting of God's energy created some such emotions or particles which created diseases, suffering, emotional disturbances, etc. And these started giving a feeling of discomfort and disturbance to God. As micro-level life was too far away, God could not reach there and solve the problem. So he would create Mahapralaya and withdraw everything into himself. This creation and withdrawal had happened several thousand times in the past.

At plane 16 the first Sun was created. Further lower planes converted this light into dense physical matter. With the massive creation of physical matter, in the course of time, outward senses became more noticeable than inner mental senses.

Awareness and power kept on reducing as creation went down from plane 0 to 31. Physical creations at plane 16 and below understood fully that their origin is from cosmic Gods from planes 0 to 15. And hence they gave themselves the names like Maya, Emptiness, shadow or mirror images

Later on, after going through twenty thousand cycles of creations and Maha Pralays, wisdom dawned on one of the Sun Moon Bright of Lotus Sutra who realised that only way to get rid of unending cycle of creation, withdrawal and recreation process is 'Only One Vehicle', of Lotus Sutra, by which one can ascend to upward Planes as Bodhisattvas.

Properties of these shadows of Gods were the same as the Gods at the plane 15. Gods as well as their shadows also subdivided further and went down up to the 31st Plane. All Shadows were supported by Gods of their original source and they were directly in communication with the God at plane 0.

Small Gods or micro life of Gods will suffer and dissolve after suffering and God will not feel bad about it. But the problem rose further. The Suffering got so intense, and a lot of emotions were involved in those sufferings that it still reached God because of the huge accumulation of sufferings. Strong and clear message from God was sent to all physical creations in Plane 16 and below that *"You are an image, or your creation is a mirage. Don't suffer for it"*.

Stars were not able to understand it and one of the stars got an idea that if I understand that creation is just an illusion, I do not reduce in size, I come back in the next birth, stronger than before, after Pralay. With this belief the Sun came back to life after Maha pralaya 25,000 times. It kept growing immensely. Other Suns looked small in comparison to Him. So this is how the seed of

Lotus Sutra or wisdom of Lotus Sutra entered from God at the 16th plane. The Wisdom was, *"Look, all your creations are out of illusion, out of shadow."* This truth was understood by one of the Suns.

Now, this Sun started expanding and thought, *"What should I do with such a big expansion?"* So he felt, let me create something which is better. So he created sons. He created Eight sons from the extra Cosmic energy that he was collecting around from the Suns, who were not able to understand that their creation was a shadow. His creation had considerably increased when compared to other Suns. He had eight Suns below him, surrounding him, rotating around him, but they were like his sons. They were produced out of his own energy. So he became the 1st Buddha. He stressed the need for creation with wisdom which did *not disturb* others. This creation of Suns rotating around him, prompted other Suns to follow the path. So he had created something which was being copied by other Suns. And this way, they found that creation which was done increased the beauty of the creation, survived and returned after the next Maha pralaya which grew further.

This wisdom was extremely important and returned after 20,000 times the effort by the first Sun. So this Wisdom was stored as a Cosmic source in Buddha, Buddha did it out of his own body energy as he was expanding. This is how the wisdom of the Lotus Sutra started.

Objective of creation of more sons of Gods is to send them to different lower planes from 16 to 31, with the clear message to **'Create with Wisdom'** which had come from God. That was the message, and whosoever creates with wisdom becomes part of LOTUS SUTRA. His energies did diminish while creating but replenished quickly due to the path of Lotus Sutra he practiced. This way, many sons of Gods started following this method and developed many Moons and Planets, and these Planets and Moons developed life. The message was penetrating deeper and deeper inside because of the eight sons of the 1st Buddha. But that also had limitations and the message of God, that CREATE WITH WISDOM that is not harmful and is beneficial to every other Sun who is connected to it, could not penetrate to the 31st level . The wisdom had to be penetrated to the 31st plane.

It necessitated the creation of another Buddha on another plane, the 24th level or the 22nd level. The message in Lotus Sutra is given in the PHANTOM CITY chapter that another Buddha descended to a lower plane. He received the message from Lotus Sutra which originated at plane no. 16, and with that wisdom, he created 16 sons. Lotus Sutra tells us that CREATION WITH WISDOM is the only energy that survives and gets stored in the Lotus Sutra and the remaining energies vanish in Maha Pralaya.

Buddha had understood this communication, and worked towards achieving that objective. All those lives which had created the *trash*, I will call it *trash - things that are not necessary for creation with wisdom, they are all trash.* They were all processed through Lotus Sutra, churned over, removed the portion which was trash, and only creative elements with wisdom were stored in them. Subsequently, only that was added to the next seed of life which came in after the Maha pralaya. This is how the growth with *Sun-Moon-bright* at plane 16 started going down to plane 22 or 24, where the Phantom City- Buddha had come. Now, this Buddha also understood the method. He had to penetrate further to the 31st plane. Hence he produced 16 children. If you read the chapter on Phantom City, it mentions that the Buddha expanded this way. One Buddha communicated wisdom. The 16 children went deeper up to the 31st plane or level and spread this message of God.

This Buddha of Phantom City had 16 sons. Their names were mentioned in Lotus Sutra. The youngest son was Gautam Buddha, who came with the power of Phantom City. His only objective was to convey the message of wisdom and to create awareness of Lotus Sutra.

If you study his life you will see that Gautam Buddha was protected from suffering initially because his father was told that when this boy grows up, he will either become a great saint if unhappy or rule the whole world if he is happy. So he was isolated from suffering in his initial stages till he was married and had a son. Now his father thought, my son has been away from suffering, and he has also married and has created a son who, of course, he will be attached to, so it will be safe for me to train him as a king so that he takes over my Empire. So he was allowed to go out, and when Gautama went out, he saw for the first time the suffering of other people.

He saw a sick person and was shocked.

He saw a dead person and was shocked.

All this was not normal because this person, Gautam, had come from a Universe where these things did not exist. So he was shocked.

Why Sickness?

Why Death?

Why Old age?

People around him did not have answers to such questions. Sickness, old age, and death for them were normal, and it was a waste of time discussing these. That was the answer he was receiving from others, and his inner soul was not ready to accept it because he knew from his past deeper communication that these were not required. So he left in a very turmoil condition to find the correct answer.

Buddha preached all his life the ways to diminish Old-Age, Suffering and Death.

His whole life went in search of that. Finally, at Bodhgaya, because of intense concentration of mind, away from all the dogmas and things that his earlier education had taught him and in that state of deeply concentrated mind absolutely in a condition when he was NOTHING- SHUNYA, he received the Communication from his father that this is what Lotus Sutra is and what his purpose, was to be in this life. "You are here to bring down this Lotus Sutra to plane no. 26".

So please understand the importance of the Lotus Sutra. Lotus Sutra has got many gates, which we call Jhanas- A wisdom entry point. You may only develop one of the wisdoms of the Lotus Sutra with which you get connected.

All those people who have taken birth on this earth are of two types:

First, those who have newly originated or have come from the Source,

Second, are those who have emerged from the previous era after surviving through the Lotus Sutra.

Those Souls who have survived through Lotus Sutra and are reborn will be advanced Souls. They will rule the earth in subsequent Mahapralaya, and that is what is happening now after Gautam Buddha descended.

You find that Earth has entered into a very different phase that was not seen before. Inventions, discoveries, and creativity of various types are returning to Earth from those who emerged from the Earth. This Earth is really becoming wonderful. As we spread the message of Lotus Sutra, all the lives that have received this message and understood even a little bit of it and are trying to link with Lotus Sutra, once connected, their energies or their Karmas that were of two types, one was creativity with wisdom and, the other was trash. - they both will start connecting with Lotus Sutra. The trash causes us old age, suffering, and death, and it makes our life very unpleasant. Even otherwise, we would have wanted to throw it out. So once we communicate with Lotus Sutra, we start shedding that trash and becoming lighter and better. Any individual, even though he might have only one Jhana or wisdom of only one gate entry point, then too, the Lotus Sutra portion of energy which that particular wisdom contains will dissolve it away and make him a little lighter. He will become light and peaceful for moments and then in that Emptiness, he will start receiving further messages from the Lotus Sutra through **Wisdom with Creativity.** The basic cause of his suffering causes him to grow in Lotus Sutra and ultimately he comes to know that the purpose of Lotus Sutra is to Create life without old age, suffering, death, etc.

Lord Christ received wisdom along with emptiness and compassion. He did some work. Allah received some wisdom with emptiness, and he too did some work. All other Gurus who have received wisdom with emptiness are being reborn as higher souls and have followers. They can spread the wisdom that they have received through several rebirths and growth or increase of life energy that comes into them.

The System has been copied in plane number 16 and is now in plane 26. It is bound to spread faster. We all somehow get connected to Lotus Sutra. Our trash will be recirculated, making us lighter and not having to go through Hell or Heaven, thereby clearing our Karmas.

Rebirth will happen because that creative energy with wisdom is the seed of life that will come back. Even if a soul clears all his Karmas of Hell and Heaven (in Lokas) by suffering after death, he takes rebirth because that is the system that Budhha has brought down to plane no. 26. But suppose he is not connected to Lotus Sutra then after Pralay, because of lack of time, his creativity with wisdom, which has not connected through Lotus Sutra may not be sufficient to survive. Lotus Sutra was never here before Buddha descended and that was what was happening on Earth. Due to this, our Earth was getting murkier and dirtier. Its pollution expanded in Hell & Heaven. That expansion of Hell & Heaven created souls, like that of Demon Master who could control ghosts to do some benefit for humanity, but he was overall, using evil energies.

In a way, he was creating but with Ignorance. Such Masters will not survive. He will also be cut down by Lotus Sutra. The method of creating fear, jealousy, hatred, etc creates so much suffering in the followers of that saint that they do not have the power to go further.

Also, People who get hold of such Masters, Tantriks, and Aghoris to manipulate others' lives are a burden to society. People whose lives are destroyed, their families curse them, and each day becomes difficult for them to carry on and survive. Only God's name keeps them afloat otherwise they would sink into a deep abyss. If such people who are in despair hold the hand of a Lotus Sutra Guru, then they regain the lost glory of their Karmas, without even harming the Evil soul. Their conscience is free from any guilt because they know they are in the safe hands of the next Avatar.

Those who have gone through the cycle of Lotus Sutra will go through the rebirth cycle, and they will always be evolving and taking rebirth in a higher form of life. Rebirth for those souls who are not in communication with Lotus Sutra will not happen ultimately in Pralay and Maha Pralay. There are many questions you may have. You may refer to Lotus Sutra, chapters Phantom City, *Sun-Moon-bright,* or the initial birth of Lotus Sutra. You must read the merging of Earth and many other chapters to know how Lotus Sutra works. *It took me approximately twenty-five years of my life to digest and practically live through it.*

Chapter 7

"But for the Lotus Sutra's sake I have been reviled and slandered,
struck with swords and staves, and sent into exile."
~Nicherin[38]

The Sword Of Kalki

I perceive myself as The Flying Horse of Kalki and sometimes as a Knight in armor with a Sword in hand. The Knight, who is the Kalki, has received a Horse that can fly. So it is a kind of Astral travel, in meditation traveling the Universe to make the eyes farsighted enough to see the visions of *ALL three worlds and the world within. When you can see the Universe, you can find your path. This means you have to get hold of the Flying Horse.*

The Sword represents the Lotus Sutra. You have the wisdom and the emptiness of Buddha. Evilness makes others suffer. When people suffer, they try to run away from it. That escape point brings them EMPTINESS. Knowingly or unknowingly, it moves or gets sucked by the *Void.* When it enters a person who has the power

38Courtesy : **Nichiren Buddhism** (Japanese: is a branch of Mahayana Buddhism based on the teachings of the 13th-century (refer Appendix pg xlviii)

of awareness with wisdom, it gets cleansed. It becomes light and flies away.

So the Sword cuts the negative energies, cleans them and cuts the head of those negative Karmas by wisdom. So the Lotus Sutra is a wisdom as Kalki has connected with Lotus Sutra by observing and traveling within with the knowledge of emptiness.

After every experience of emptiness, he sees a different realm. Sometimes he sees the 16th plane, sometimes the 15th, sometimes the 14th and so on. Only after he empties the 16th plane, can he see the 15th. Buddha teaches this. **Whosoever has this Flying Horse, the Sword of Lotus Sutra, the wisdom can remove all types of negativity. This is the system of KALKI.**

The representation of my spiritual progress over the years can be summarised as follows: In

1937.....Horse

1951.....rider on the Horse (shooting star with penetrating awareness)

1992.....Horse is operated to grow flying wings by Narayana

1994......growing of Wings starts

2017......the rider is awarded a weapon that will grow as the Sword of Kalki

2022......the Sword has grown long enough to slay the Evil from a distance

2047..... Kalki will have a full-fledged Sword and fast-riding Horse with long wings

And the creation will start becoming free from all evilness and diseases, there will be no need for doctors, medicines, police, lawyers, judges, army, or weapons. There will be no visas or passports.

My Spiritual Progress as Per Human Analogy of Avatars:

Dec 1936.. Seed of life ....fish.......tortoise

Mar 1937....Monkey with a tail

July 1937....Lion

Aug 1937...Bauna, an underdeveloped human body 1951........Parashurama ..an emotional human being

1963........Role of Ram

1972........Krishna born

1992.......preparation for Buddhahood

1994.......entry to Buddhahood .start of Bodhisattva 2017.......Bodhisattva.Entry to Kalkihood

2047.......Kalki arrival

Divine Guidance & Visions

After repeatedly entering Hell, meeting ghosts, and cleaning them for the last 15 years, approximately at the age of 80, I had acquired many diseases in my body. I have talked about those diseases. The result was that I was discharged from the hospital to die peacefully at home, and then death occurred. Just before dying, my heart complained that my suffering was so much that I was *losing my awareness*, and I was promised that I would never lose it so that I could continue my job in the next birth. The complaint came from within, followed by a vision. I will speak of the vision now.

There was a blue expanse of sky, and there was light everywhere beyond the vast sky. That light was God. Below the light and vast space were two platforms. One at a higher level and the other at a lower level. At the higher level, there were many personalities, saints in long gray gowns, and on the lower platform again, there were many saints who were wearing long white robes. In between these two platforms, in the middle, was a mediator. A Booming voice of God came out of the light from beyond and said,

This person here has a complaint that he has died ***without*** *awareness.*

I had promised him that if he kept the Sword of Lotus Sutra with him, He would never lose his awareness, but he says the suffering is so severe that he has lost his awareness. Whose mistake is this?

The mediator replied, saying this person was given 5th-level protection. The voice from beyond roared,

You are wrong. He should have been given Zero-Level Protection.

Soon after that, my vision ended. I woke up from that vision and later on heard my Guru's voice,

"Now you have been given Zero-Level Protection, throw away all your medicines and painkillers. You will recover day by day and will live for 25 or more years. You have a lot of work in this existence. There are other options too. If you do not want to live for 25 years because your body is weak at present, then you will gain the capability to transform your soul into some other body and continue with your work up to 2047. And then this world will be 80% free from sufferings and pain of death and mental agonies".

Later, when I asked, what this white and gray-robed army of saints and mediator meant, I was told,

The mediator has sacrificed his life to elongate yours by 25 years or more.

The saints in Grey are God elements. They are the sons of Gods. The saints in White robes are Buddhas, and they are formed from creation.

The other name for creation is emptiness. So what is this emptiness? I was told that when God's sons divided further and came up to the 15th plane, they were not happy with the creation adequately as desired, so God extended that creation by creating a mirror image of Himself at 16th level. It is not God but an image of Himself. It may be like a reflection in the mirror or like a Shadow of God. The nature of this creation is the same as God. It can divide, subdivide, mix, intermingle, and create.

The white-robed saints that you saw were Buddhas who have evolved from creation, and grey-robed saints are sons of God. Every time a God enters into the form of an avatar in creation, and if he is not capable enough to achieve the objective fully, he gets lost or mixed up in creation. If he is wisdom-oriented, he is careful, and if he comes back, he comes back with wisdom. All those who formed the principles of the Lotus Sutra accumulated this wisdom and they kept it in store. Any God who enters as Avatar and takes that accumulated wisdom, that is the Sword of Lotus Sutra, with him, is not supposed to get lost in creation. That is exactly what I was supposed to be.

I came down with a promise that I am going to take the *Sword of Lotus Sutra* with me in this existence and take the form of an Avatar. But there was a mistake in communication. The power source in between misjudged me. As I had descended from Plane 5 to Plane 26, he thought it fit for me to be awarded with 5th level protection. However, considering the risks involved in the task I was assigned, God awarded me zero level protection and sent me back to continue with my life.

I got trained to enter the world of evil and clean it. Before that, I was given an experience of black Spirits, ghosts, and negative elements in the form of small to large ghosts entering my body. I was ready to go to Hell each time and fight back against evil, thereby reducing the intensity of evil on Earth. That is how and why when I go to bed every night, I enter the zone of ghosts, which is Hell. The ghosts try to enter the emptiness in me because they are suffering there. My body allows them to enter, in the sense that it is not aware. My body would fill with their negative energies, and that would cause pain. I would wake up suddenly due to the pain and sit for meditation, clearing those pains and sufferings. I had been doing this process for the past 15 yrs. That means I have been fighting the evil world in my own way, even twice or thrice a day. It was like- Going to sleep, entering evil zones, finding and clearing the ghosts and other evil souls. That is what I used to call meditation.

Every individual who is in a spiritual journey has to experience the dark forces, in his lifetime, to reach his ultimate path. This is the law of Universal Path. Your life perspective gets changed drastically. You face [39]Spiritual Emergencies and you are thrown out of your comfort zone. Part of your spiritual awakening process involves connecting you with the forces of the unconscious mind or "Spirit realm" which you have not yet learned to navigate. Furthermore, having our mystical experiences dismissed as being purely 'psychotic,' 'borderline,' or 'schizophrenic' not only denies the spiritual validity of what we're going through but also adds an unnecessary element of fear and terror to the experience. This fear and terror can be profoundly crippling and can make the whole

---

39(courtesy) https://lonerwolf.com/spiritual-emergency/#

experience much more difficult than it really needs to be.

Cosmic Love is absolutely ruthless and highly indifferent,
it teaches its lessons whether you like/dislike them or not.
~ John Lilly[40]

I continued with my task of entering Hell and allowed ghosts to enter my body and freed them from their evilness but in turn, took their sufferings onto myself. At times I felt very sick and old. As stated earlier, I died due to the process but came back to life after receiving upgraded Zero-level protection. With the higher protection, I could go deeper into Hell and continue with my task of relieving ghosts from their evilness. With meditation, I cured myself and continued with my task. I had the satisfaction of relieving the ghosts from their evilness, thus slowly cleaning Hell. In turn, I took their sufferings and got cured by the power of meditation. However, my major objective was to find my daughter Gitu and I was willing to go through any hardship to achieve this. I have been on this task since I was 80 years old. Due to the Zero Level Protection I had, ghosts could not harm me and I had better control over them. I always succeeded in my task and

---

40(courtesy) https://www.goodreads.com/quotes/3279260-cosmic-love-is-absolutely-ruthless-and-highly-indifferent-it-teaches

recovered quickly after taking their sufferings onto me in the process of relieving them from Hell. My health has improved, I have almost stopped all medicines, and I look much better.

I kept on entering Hell in search of Gitu. At last, in June end, 2022, I succeeded in my task of finding her. It took almost 5years of relentless search - at times even 3 times in a day I was on this task. I am glad that Gitu is now at a safe level and she is free from all suffering of the past. Incidentally, I came to know that the evil master, the Master of those ghosts, who was instrumental in giving me the experience of several ghosts, who could hear my Inner voice and control my body and even kill me, died in the first week of June 2022. I am continuing with my task of cleaning the Hell.

This Earth is very dangerous for the human body. Whoever takes birth, doesn't know where life will take them. My younger daughter recently asked me as to why Gitu had to die when her Karmas were not so bad to put her in such a horrible situation. I explained to her that the world is a very dangerous place and it has to be changed and purified. That is the work I have taken up.

Plane numbers 0 to 15 are ruled by the most powerful God at Zero level, with the highest level of awareness. Plane numbers 16 to 31 come under the rule of Kalki with the sword of Lotus Sutra and winged horse of Buddha. As Kalki goes down the level from 16th to 17th level he acquires a longer and stronger sword as well as a faster horse. In other words Kalki's power and speed keeps increasing as he keeps going each level from 16th to 31st level. We are on plane 26. Plane 27 will have short human life, but the *Kalki of that Era will have a longer Sword and a faster Horse*. This will be an advanced Kalki compared to the Kalki of our plane.

Method Of Meditation As Per Lotus Sutra

In ancient times, when Earth was not uninhabited, Heaven was heavily occupied by Gods, Devis and Devtas. Here I am referring to the upper planes as Heaven - not the Heaven attached to the Loka. Upper and Lower Lokas were created later on when creation was established on Earth and Karmas were accumulated.

Our present existence is at the 7th Chakra through our Navel which is the 3rd Chakra from base, which is our source. As a child, we were connected with the umbilical cord of our Mother from the Navel point, while those Gods, Devi, and Devtas were at a higher level.

They could meditate and go to the top Crown Chakra and finally back to the source. They gain nothing in this process. Some of them when they rise, chakra by chakra and get powers that are not available in that plane, those powers pull them back to creation and they start enjoying the benefits of creation. So we say that they have lost their way. In reality, they have not lost their way. They make mistakes when they are in creation because of lack of wisdom and they suffer. Ultimately they gain wisdom. Creation wants to give us *wisdom with experience.* Some want to escape by going through the method of Chakras. Fortunately on Earth, which is at the 7th Chakra, I have gone through the whole history of evolution. Few have been able to go to Crown Chakra successfully. Many of them have risen in their Chakras, gained powers, used them to achieve their selfish goals, and fallen back.

Now, this is what creation is teaching us. *Gaining wisdom is ultimate learning. Creation wants wisdom.* In the first chapter itself, Lotus Sutra disapproves of the method of Meditation that our ancient yogis followed. I have come to the conclusion that such a method of meditation was appropriate at higher planes but at our present level, it is not proper. Our ancient Rishis and Munis were at a higher plane and so they were successful in achieving their goal of salvation.

So the method that Lotus Sutra suggests is, like Fish wanting to become a tortoise to walk on land, had to make an effort to change the body. Fish had to develop legs, it had to develop the shell on its back so that stones do not hurt them. *Evolution is a continuous process of changes taking place in many directions. We meditate on emptiness. We experience emptiness in every chakra, so we are not bothered about which chakra we are in. We just meditate so that our thoughts, our sensations, our sickness, and our sufferings, go away and we are peaceful. We feel as if nothing is there. We experience emptiness.* After we experience emptiness, we will necessarily feel our ego is false. 'I' ego collects all these attributes, which are removed, and ego dissipates in emptiness. Our physical body too will change to face the new challenges. Weak organs will regenerate and health will improve to a great extent.

So the wisdom that we all are one, comes first. We collect enormous energy in our body while meditating and experiencing emptiness. That energy gets restored in our body and we have to go back to creation. That means to rise from meditation and get involved in day-to-day activities. After we get involved in the day-to-day activities we face problems of the creation. And then we forget our path, we get involved in them, we try to solve them and gain some wisdom. Again we go back to meditation. In this process of experiencing the emptiness and experiencing the creation, you are collecting wisdom.

With this method of meditation, ***you are now diverting the energies horizontally towards a shield around your body, instead of ascending on chakras.*** The shield around our body is invisible to our eyes which is called *Wisdom Shield- Dharam Kaya* in Buddhism. When you are doing some creative work, one more halo gets created around your body. This halo is called Nirman kaya in Buddhism. In that state neither negative nor positive thoughts come to you.

When you are extremely engrossed in creation and you are very peaceful, that is called *Nirmaan Kaya*. So all the energy you are collecting through meditation by experiencing the emptiness now gets diverted to either *Nirman Kaya (Creativity) or Dharma Kaya (Wisdom)* if you are experiencing other people's troubles and taking time to solve those. These two Kayas you are developing are changing your physical form which is generally not visible, but you are changing. You are getting connected to Lotus Sutra. This is the gauge towards connection to Lotus Sutra.

Lotus Sutra calls you **Bodhisattva**. Yes, that means a Bodhisattva is the one who starts ***diverting his energy from chakras to creation.*** If you rise in chakras you gain powers, but because you have no wisdom you fall. In this case, you will rise as much as you go up in chakras but you will rise carefully with wisdom. Because wisdom is also rising in you and that will guide you further.

So there is no falling. This is the ONLY ONE VEHICLE. THERE IS NO OTHER METHOD available that can make you rise and stay at that level. Both methods have the same objective but with the first method, you are rising on a millimeter scale while the target is kilometers away. You are bound to be unstable in this long process but now you are supported by a solid base and are steadily rising above. You will not fall. If your *Nirman Kaya & Dharm Kaya* around your body are strong enough these give you prosperity, happiness, and what you desire. But you use it judiciously with wisdom and in the wisdom, you also know the experience of emptiness that you are ALL ONE. *So you start contributing your prosperity and happiness to others by way of financial or physical help. Help can also be rendered in the form of advice on different matters like medical, health, finance, and even personal advice. Help others in every way as you feel connected because of the final wisdom of emptiness.* When you do that the third form of Kaaya forms around you and that is called *Sambhog Kaaya.* The effect of *Sambhog Kaaya* is that you are increasing your bank balance of Merits. You are helping others and in fact, you are giving away your share of wealth, happiness, etc., but in return, you are getting the *Sambhog Kaaya Shield.* Dharmas, the truth, do not dissolve anytime. You have done good, it will come back to you. It will not go away anywhere. Your goodness gets stored because you do not require it. Later on, whenever needed that reservoir of *Sambhog Kaya* comes and gives you relief. If you are accustomed to luxury living because of the abundance of *Sambhog Kaya* and there is enough storage in *Sambhog Kaaya,* even a crisis will not change your lifestyle. So this is the method. There is no other better method available to You.

http://www.cttbusa.org/lotus/lotus_contents.asp[41]

Once you have started this method of Meditation you are changing your body from Krishna to Buddha level. And when you are on this path which is a very long one, you are called a Bodhisattva. By default, the Bodhisattvas get a special place when they die, which prevents them from going into annihilation when the Yug ends. There is a period of Maha Pralaya at the end of Maha Yuga. Our Earth also experiences Maha Pralaya which brings an end to all life but these Bodhisattvas who are connected to Lotus Sutra go back to the pool of Lotus Sutra and they would be lying there for whatever period of Maha Pralaya. When the next creation starts they will be born again in an appropriate Era as they are far ahead of those who are coming to life for the first time in the new creation. Bodhisattvas have the experience of the past creation.

41(Courtesy http://www.cttbusa.org/lotus/lotus_contents.asp)

They have also collected *Sambhog Kaya, Nirman Kaya, and Dharam Kaya.* That's a very big leap. They will be recognized as highly advanced people.

In Satyug, life will start again from fish and develop up to the level of Krishna and then to Bodhisattva and Buddhas. But you are already a Bodhisattva. So you will wait till that Era comes and take over. That is the advantage of your becoming a Bodhisattva. This advantage is not available up to the Krishna level. This advantage is only available in Lotus Sutra. Hence, once again, I repeat that this is the ***only One Vehicle*** that can make you go up. No other system can help you.

Now that I have explained the importance of the Lotus Sutra our Vedas also mention the next step, which is *Kalkihood.* The process of changing from Buddha to Kalki is a process that is not available to us because we have two products with us. One is God and the other is Creation. To become Buddha we have to reach the highest level of creation and the second element is God in us who is already at the top of creation. When we have both God and creation of the topmost levels in us, we will go back to our source with full force and wisdom of creation. That is the Ultimate Path and that is what God is doing to our bodies and our life. Every one of us is contributing to that. So remember, *Kalkihood is the final process when a Kalki comes through an Avatar and he comes with a flying horse and the sword of Lotus Sutra with him. He goes to the level from human being to Buddha and then he becomes Kalki. He is the one who inhales the whole of the Creation through the Lotus Sutra back to its Source. He is the one who will create the Maha Pralaya but not immediately. First, the negativities and blackness have to go, which in turn will eliminate suffering. Creation has to get a full force of power. Creation has to come up to the best level possible by the life that exists at that time. This same creation which has gone to the best level will move ahead in the next Era.*

Kalki comes only when God comes down as an Avatar. And If you can see Kalki in this existence, remember sooner or later you will join Him. You have to be a part of Him because whether you want it or not Maha Pralaya will bring you to that state. The sooner you join Kalki, the faster you will rise because now you have the power and wisdom of Kalki of Lotus Sutra. You will rise and become a high-level Bodhisattva. By the time the era ends you will be a high-level Bodhisattva in the chain of Lotus Sutra for the next creation.

The Vicious Attack

As narrated earlier, my family members were also attacked in the past. When I fell and broke my back, my wife too had a fall and broke her leg and she was in plaster for 2 months and suffered a lot. My other daughter went through seeming visions from Hell after the death of her sister.

My current strong meditation indicates that a special chapter or a book should be written coming out openly against the attacks that had caused misery to my family.

My deceased daughter, who had been going through some suffering and pain for the last 15 years because of this vicious attack, is slowly recovering due to the Shakti that appears in my body to fight back. Shakti is instrumental in my success as well as in my family's safety without which we all could not have survived. Shakti, which had been working for 15 years, was also quite strong and very capable of handling such vicious attacks. In this way, we can also conclude that this Shakti is capable of succeeding in the huge task of abolishing Hell and Heaven.

We, all as a family, try to be instrumental in helping others, by removing the negative energies surrounding the Universe. Here 'family' refers to the group of ghosts I had cleansed and liberated. I had seen the majority of liberated ghosts and Spirits help in my task of finding hide-out of such other ghosts. Outwardly you do not see us working, but inwardly through awareness and emptiness, we free the restless hungry ghosts by cleansing and liberating them.

Chapter 8

"My world of science and logic has turned upside down,
the asuras and devas are as real as the earth beings,
one of the devas might be my ancestor! "[42]

Transition To Kalki

Sometimes, a big thing happens that creates a shock wave in society. The reason for the waves being created is due to sudden and drastic changes introduced in the system. Whatever I have stated here is nothing but the truth. Writing this book was against my thought because neither our society nor my family nor the people surrounding me, might be able to face and accept it. It is a very controversial topic and hurts the sentiments of many of my family members. No doubt the truth will prevail. Nobody can prevent the truth from being brought forward, it has to come out in the open. Presently it may not come out so openly because the waves and their effects may not be strong, but with time, it will.

My children told me to write it down and publish my experience and spread the message for the benefit of people who opt to know the truth of creation in further

42 (Courtesy : Sword of Kalki - (Pl click 'more' to read further)

depth. It will be a silent process. The book will be in the public domain without propaganda. The book which is written from my recorded messages and its manuscript will be with me, or in my family's safe custody.

Many years later, if needed, this book will come up again and benefit all future generations. I still confirm that whatever has happened inside my body for the last twenty-thirty years has been put down by me explicitly and I can visualize the mystery behind it and express it. Some of it I have spoken about, and some is still inside me. It is so deep inside, still, it is fine and I would like to keep this manuscript safe without exposing the emotional upheaval it will create in my family. I will keep it safely with my family. I will keep this book safe for future generations. If required further, the content of Part 2 of the book is being prepared, explaining more details and will be published at an appropriate time post the release of this book to the public.

Let us understand the problems on Earth scientifically.

Why are there Hell and Heaven-Lokas?

What complications have they caused?

Why were they formed?

How come our Rishis, Munis, and saints who went to the Himalayas for thousands of years found different solutions? But the real problem was totally different.

The first Vision I had during meditation in the past, which I treat as the most important in my life, gave me an insight into two basic things active on earth:

One is God who wants to Create.

Second is creation, the one God has created.

God has created this creation out of copying his life, his energy, or a shadow of his life. It is a mirror image of his Life. It has the same properties of division, subdivision, and sections as this creation had.

When Buddhas who were a part of creation started searching, they found very good methods which helped them rise. They created the ladder of Lotus Sutra which was the one that could make them climb up and ultimately they reached the top. They found nothing there. So they named it LOTUS, **Emptiness**, or Shunyata. But the Gods who created this creation knew that it is a mirror image of the creation. So they called it Maya or creation. The one which has no real substance. They approached it with different names. Creation cannot be treated as nothing or dirt, because almost everything we are made of is out of creation. Our senses are the product of creation but it has limitations. Our physical senses cannot realize God but can understand the creation of God.

After the end of each life cycle, saints who meditated were sent back to the center for a reason i.e. Godliness back from where they started their journey. But when creation found an easy method of rising from any level to a higher level, which we can call **Emptiness** or Nothingness[43], they understood the importance of creation and the ladder they had created. This Earth is very complicated. It had gone into complications due to the continuous growth of negative energies and their positive energies intertwining amongst each other.

These got so complicated that humanity started facing huge suffering. Crisis, world wars, destruction, completion of era, and creation of a new era all continued, and the troubles started mounting.

To ensure the survival of creation, a zone of separation was created between active creation and a creation that was sleeping. These separated zones are called Hell and Heaven or in short *Lokas*. Hell and Heaven are abrasions. These are not appropriate creations. These are products that create delay in the play of Karmas. *Justice gets delayed because we have Hell and Heaven.* Karmas which want to work on our body immediately but are not able to do it, get deposited in Hell and then Heaven at different periods. So when people or creation see each other and they see bad people prospering and good people suffering, they get further puzzled. I have seen many families destroyed by the ghosts and Spirits which forcibly occupy the human body and create havoc in the family and their destructive effect goes on for Generations. So these Spooks, these Spirits, these Goblins, these Ghosts who

---

43 Courtesy: (ref Pg 337 of LS book)

are supposed to be in isolation in Hell. ***Because of the excessive pressure, they had been entering the lives of people and creating crisis.*** If we want our creation to improve to a positive level, we have to go back to the original set up when there was no Lokas, As mentioned earlier, Lokas were brought in, to accommodate souls with excessive accumulated Karmas as a buffer zone. That means Ghosts and Souls to be cleansed, liberated and Hell and Heaven to be destroyed. They have to be completely abolished. This is a very difficult task as Hell and Heaven (Lokas) had been filling up for Billions of years, generation after generation which is wide spread.

Now how to destroy them? *At the end of Maha Yuga, creation of Kalki, whom we call the tenth Avatar is necessitated. He has the support of the Lotus Sutra and the wisdom of the Buddha. When Lotus Sutra falls in the hands of Kalki, who originated from the level of God, has all the wisdom that is accumulated and required in this creation, and with the support of wisdom, he develops further strengths and then he attacks Hell. Heaven gets automatically destroyed when Hell gets destroyed because these are both negative and positive entities and they emerge from the same source. As the intensity of Hell goes down, the intensity of Heaven also diminishes.*

How does Kalki do this? This is a technical process. It is an extremely difficult and complex process. Kalki has to develop the science to see Hell and see the ghosts. The present senses are not suitable for that, He has to develop extra senses. *To create those extra senses he has to go into deep meditation within and create an abundance of strong power in the senses of feeling that he has so that he can see Hell & Heaven which originate from the body itself.* So first he has to develop his inner eyes for seeing Hell. Then he has to see the cause of the formation of Hell, which is easily known to many people. They know these are our *desire*s. These are our negative emotions of Hell, fear, hate, and many more negative things. Not only do they create Hell in our body when we live, but even after death, these become a part of Hell which accumulates karmas. Even good deeds which people practice accumulate and go to Heaven. This is how the creation of Hell and Heaven takes place in the body.

While we are alive all Karmas are to be cleared. They do not cancel each other. Evil Karmas are heavy and after death, they appear first. Good Karmas are light. They come later.

Our Earth is now in Plane 26. There will be many cycles of four Yugas. At the end of each cycle, Kalki will come and the Mahayuga will end. Same cycle will repeat on Plane 27 and 28 also.

As mentioned in Chapter 1,

0 to 31 planes Total of 32 planes exist. And our earth is on the 26th plane.

0 to 15 .....God's planes

16 to 31...... Planes of **Emptiness**.

Life on plane 27 level will be compact. The maximum life expectancy will be around 30 years instead of 100 years on earth at plane 26. They will accomplish more than what we do in 100 years.

When life at plane 26 is perfected, Pralaya (gap in time) will occur. And then life will evolve at plane 27. Gods at 15th level created their images at 16th level. Along with these images Gods from 15th level could move around at 16th level. This process continued at lower planes as well and their awareness level kept diminishing as they went down each level. So the awareness at plane 31 will be the least. On Plane 17 life was further increasing. At plane 26 it is in millions. At plane 27 it will be billions. On planes 28 to 31, we do not know. Lotus Sutra mentions fast and short life span on plane 27.

Kalki has not only to develop the senses to see this creation in the body but he has to also develop an extra sense to dissolve them in the body. So the Tenth avatar, God who we named Kalki, enters the body of a creation of this Earth. Now when he selects a body, he knows that he has the experience. He starts working on this body. First, he creates a sight through which he can see Hell and Heaven (Lokas) that had been created earlier, and then he works towards achieving a higher experience to dissolve Hell & Heaven portions that are in the body.

The same thing happened to me. I experienced different types of ghosts which I mentioned earlier. The very light ones, then the ones which were at medium level, who could control my body, actions, and movements. The worst ones can kill you.

So, if I wanted to develop as a Kalki, I had to develop the sight to see those ghosts in my body, and secondly, I had to develop the power to dissolve them. When I could dissolve these in my body, I could then enter Hell with a little bit of boldness because I had the experience.

Unfortunately, my daughter was taken away by those ghosts and I had a strong desire to rescue her. So I had a valid reason to enter Hell without fear of my life and that's why I started my mission, in search of my daughter.

Once I started going to Hell, I found it easier to go deeper and deeper, with the background of my gained experiences and increased determination to locate my daughter.

My encounter with Ghost Guru or Master, which I referred to before, was not accidental but the result of my destiny, and the experience I gained there helped in my mission to scan Hell in search of my lost daughter and to cleanse the place to start with.

I had been on this mission for the last fifteen to twenty years. Every day I would enter and destroy as many as I could but return with damages to my physical body. That is the process I had gone through.

I hence refer to all **Ghost Gurus. or any Guru who manipulates your destiny or Karmas, to suit their self-interest- as Master, they are not Gurus**, as in India the term Guru holds a lot of respect. The highest Guru God comes with the name of Kalki. He has the power of **Emptiness** and also of compassion. Kalki is shown as riding a Horse with a Sword in hand and the Horse has wings. The Sword represents the Compassion part. Compassion is a very important part of the Lotus Sutra. The riding horse with wings represents the development of Buddhahood. The development of individuals into Buddha hood. Wings and their size represent the growth in Buddhahood. The length of the Sword also represents the Lotus Sutra power of compassion that one carries. If you look at the history of our Earth, the Lotus Sutra came 2600 years back, and then Lord of Compassion Jesus Christ came to uplift the downtrodden. **Emptiness is at the highest level and Compassion is lower.** So Buddha came with **Emptiness**. But Gautam Buddha was a son of Buddha who brought the Lotus Sutra. Christ came with compassion. Then **Emptiness** God came as Allah.

The Master of the Devil who utilizes negative power to bring people on the right path is that Ghost Master that I faced. There are many Gods of Love in this Yuga. Karnataka seer who has been arrested or Asaram or other Gurus who have fallen prey to love/lust. *Love comes below **Emptiness** and Compassion levels.* And Devil Gurus- Master comes still lower. The highest Guru is one who has both compassion and **Emptiness** and that is Kalki.

Disciples do grow spiritually, but due to their insights and transformations, and not because of the false Guru. It is not the teacher but the spiritual seeker, who holds all the cards finally. So calling them Guru insults the RESPECT the word Guru holds, since olden times.

That's why, I have named the bad Guru as MASTER, and not as GURU.

In writing this book, three major levels of actors are working:

1. The Shakti inside me.

2. My friend's Guru, who had the control and power of many Spirits and ghosts.

3. My family members- Poonam, Renu, Gitu, I and Guru Prasad are all at the lower level.

These three types of characters are involved in developing this book. All three, look at this book from different perspectives. Now let us go in-depth to understand this. Because the reasoning of each of the above three is different, the book's flow will be suitable for those depending on your receptivity, or Guru, or my inner self to understand.

Let me explain it differently. Let us see all 3 views. Like, I play Golf daily. The ball is aimed to go into a pit hole when hit even from a long distance in as few strokes as possible. In between the striking point and the target, there may be unsettled terrain, uneven grass surface, stones, higher areas, small drains, dunes, and many obstacles.

1. If God or Shakti wants to hit the ball, as he has more power, he will hit the ball far, crossing mountains, valleys, plants, trees, etc. if he so wishes. But as it cannot see the hole, it might hit an unknown place and not be visible or it could be very near the hole.

2. The friend's Guru-The Master. He has few extra powers. He will hit the ball far as compared to an ordinary man, but not as far as my Inner voice. He sees the obstacles like valleys and drains and hopes he will cross them easily hoping that it will quietly follow the path on which he has set it to. But there is no limit to probabilities and it might harm someone around. It might hit a stone, or a mountain and it ultimately does not give much success. Sometimes it crosses these obstacles and gets some benefits. That is the state of that Master.

3. We, ordinary human beings, have lesser power. We have little idea of how far the hole is. We can see the mountain but not the drains, stones, valleys, and such far-away obstacles.

Depending on the level of our power, we play with our perceptions, vision, and experiences. Writing this book is a similar concept. We are writing. Shakti says to cut the mountains and level the drains, to make the Hole visible, and to hit the ball to reach the target or at least near it. Blindly, in darkness, if I hit the ball, it may cross the mountains and the boulders but it might strike at some other place too. These mountains, drains and other obstacles are a nuisance!

Similarly, Hell & Heaven are troublesome to cross. Finish it off. Shakti of my Inner Guru does not want the Zones of Hell and Heaven to create obstacles in our lives so that wisdom can directly penetrate the small Spirits and Atmas who have the sense to understand it or ears to listen to it. That voice doesn't resound after hitting stones or resonate or does not get diverted.

So let us study the Guru, Master's power, or Shakti. The power of the Master is not so effective. But he has more strength than me. He will also try to improve his power. Efforts made by all three are to reach the target, create impact and yield positive results. All three, My Inner voice, Master, or ordinary human beings reach the goal. We might reach it after 50 strokes. Shakti might reach in one stroke. Guru may reach in one or 50 strokes, but all would succeed and reach.

We have to understand the system behind it. The Shakti wants to remove Hell and Heaven zones. So it sacrificed itself, took the form of the Kalki with his powerful wisdom and weapon, and eliminated all obstacles on the path by removing the mountains and valleys to reach the target. This is something we must understand.

Generally, ordinary people avoid fighting with such Demon Masters even if they want to save and protect their near and dear ones as they fear that the Master can attack them with his evil power. This is all nonsense. This thinking is due to the ignorance of people. I see only the goal. Ordinary people have limited knowledge. I, along with the Lotus Sutra, have the power to level or tone down these hurdles. We try to help others and the Universe at large, in the way explained above.

I have saved thousands of ghosts in the past 15 years. My method is simple. First I create an **Emptiness** in my body. Demons who are going through unbearable suffering in Hell enter the **Emptiness** in my body and I help them by clearing their suffering with the cooperation of my body.

The second method is a difficult one. Suppose any of my near and dear ones have some effect of a ghost, I use my desire/ wish that I put in my ***Emptiness*** *to attract the demon affecting my family and take it in my body. I have the power to pull such demons who are not willing to cooperate, into my body and then clear their evil intentions by taking their sufferings onto my body. My method cannot harm any life.* That is the specialty of this method. Even if I wish to harm them, I cannot. That is why from the beginning and after knowing Gitus' suffering I never tried to harbor negative feelings towards the Master. I would just say that he is doing it out of ignorance. And leave it at that. Because of his ignorance, he needs to be taken care of. His powers had to be reduced. I had the method and I used it. My basic intention in mind was to help him, not to harm him because my daughter, Gitu was suffering. This has to be understood. Any ghost or demon either agrees to enter my body out of free will or if it doesn't want to come, it need not come. Even if he comes into my body it has full freedom to leave anytime. Only those who try to be aggressive and work against my desire to try and save my daughter in Hell, these demons which entered my body to cripple and weaken me, had to be changed, not destroyed. Their evilness and aggressiveness had to be controlled. Such evil powers had to be cleansed so that they do not harbor or create obstacles to my path of wisdom. They come into my body because of their Master. They first tried their best to follow their Guru's wish until they became very weak. By entering my body they realized that they were becoming free from their sufferings and found an escape route to free themselves from the Master. What they did after that is not my concern. They might have gone back to the Guru or they might have gone to freedom it is for each of them to decide.

Fight between Ghost Master & Emptiness

The Ghost Master is Lord of Adi Lokas. He has over a long period of time developed so many skills and those skills are so creative that he became a master of all the Lokas. Those powers that he had developed, were able to penetrate human-life on Earth. He would take birth on Earth as a Human body and the skills that he had developed, made him the Master of the Lokas. He could destroy any human being. Imagine that the minimum power that he had was that with the help of any ghost, he could read the mind of any person or human body. Not only that, he could read the mind of the person and give him a verbal reply, which will shock and impress the person but he could manipulate the mind and not to imagine that he had the skills to take over ghost power and manipulate the body of a human being. The body will NOT obey the mind of the human being. But will obey the ghost who is in control of Ghost Master. Further, he had the power to **kill** a person and bring him as a member in his own world of Lokas. Ghost Master was not a small entity. He had developed the world through millions of years in the Lokas and created this power. This made him feel like not only God of Lokas but also God of Earth. Now the same story can be converted to explain a drop of water and cloud and the Sun and **Emptiness** behind it.

A drop of water is like a GHOST MASTER who had developed so many skills that he could control all the ghosts in the Lokas. Same way the drop of water knowing its nature would consider itself as a part of the whole sea.

'Look, the whole Sea belongs to me, I am the Master of the Sea', thought the drop of water because he was exceptional. Now this drop of water assumes that his power has created life on Earth, all these human beings, animals, plants, everything to the evolution of

Fish and ten avatars. He feels he is God, this mere drop of water!!!

The Ghost Master is like this drop of water and feels he can challenge the **Emptiness**. Challenge between this Ghost Master who faced the emptiness in the body of Ram Peswani, was the same story. The result is incomparable. Whatever the water may be, or whatever the Ghost Master may feel that they are Gods or that they have got mighty powers but compared to emptiness they are nothing.

Now the same is the story of a drop of water. A drop of water challenges emptiness. It does not know that emptiness is the creator of Suns. The Suns had created clouds and this cloud contains water. That drop of water when it tries to face the emptiness, in fact it is directly challenging the Sun. Emptiness can CREATE AS many Suns as it can. Already this one drop of water does not know how mighty the Suns are because the Sun is far away and looks like a small globe of light and the drop of water sees the seas occupying almost more than three-fourth portions of the Earth!!! What this drop of water sees, is different from his actual position.This is that story of Ghost Master. Ghost Master was trying to control the whole Earth and the Lokas. Considering himself as the future God and when emptiness saw how much confusion and chaos this Ghost Master is creating, it had to teach him a lesson. Because emptiness had entered to finish all the Lokas and Ghost Master was one of the energies which was trying to increase the power of Lokas. conflict was going to happen and it happened.

Let us assume a big Cloud is in the sky and it wants to lighten itself by raining. That one Unit of Cloud will pour down on Earth in many- many thousands of drops. Every drop supposing has an Ego. One drop says "I am A", another says "I am B", third one says "I am C", in this way every drop has named itself as per the Ego. Now the funny issue is that drops will stay on Earth and that cloud will be in sky.

Cloud is in a state of happiness, is light, moves around, has no smell, or dirt, and is in a state of pure bliss. Whereas these drops, all screaming "I am" are stuck on earth's dirt. The subconscious desire of the drops is to become the Cloud but they cannot because they have big egos and are stuck there forever. Therefore Lotus Sutra says to go in emptiness, nothingness, void, or shunyata. Make yourself so conscious or increase your state of understanding so that whenever the thought "I am" arises, it gets dissolved with understanding.

"I am A"...remove that A,

"I am B"... remove that B,

"I am C"...remove C.

When we remove our names, we find ourselves.

You should attain the state where you are not bothered about who is with whom or who is in whose body. The fact is that if the ego of A is light, the ego of C is also light then the drops can all become one. That way they can become one because they made themselves light.

When all the drops become light, then they can become a cloud. When all the egos of the world start caring about the happiness and sadness of others as their own, then they all unite and get light and can float in the sky as a cloud. ***This is the only road as shown by the Lotus Sutra, it is the only Vehicle of Lotus Sutra, where we all can once again become THE CLOUD.*** These millions of drops when united, in that state when together they become a cloud , each drop's desires get fulfilled. This becomes possible when our desire gets separated from the rest and the ego vanishes. You can say it to be like a collective or mass prayer or universal chanting for desperate liberation from EVILNESS.

I have been doing deep meditation for a few decades now. I experience the state of emptiness and ***then I lose it, thousands of times, due to my worldly attitude towards it. But with each understanding and experiencing Emptiness, I gained too, when I absorbed other's ego. To understand this process, you have to experience the state of EMPTINESS which is very necessary***. At every step, and every moment, experiencing the state of emptiness in meditation is required. Once you experience EMPTINESS, a miracle happens, magic happens. This is an important point to understand in Lotus Sutra.

That Ghost Master I referred to earlier was in a state of "I am...". He was indeed harming others but he thought he was doing them good. He was doing so in the state of "I am..."

Ghost Master, considered himself to be a very powerful God. But he was in the state of " I am". When one is in a state of 'I am..", he is just a drop of water in the ocean. He was dealing with a person having an enriched experience of emptiness or shunyata which is like a drop of water trying to control a cloud. He did not realise that the cloud had the power to suck that drop of water. However the result was that Ghost Master could not distinguish between the cloud and drop of water, he rather faced the consequences of reduction in his powers.

Without any further hurdle, I could move out of that Ashram. With no ego in me, enmity, hatred, and pain all got lost in the air. That is the magic of EMPTINESS, the magic of entering Shunyata.

EGO is not positive but very harmful. The feeling of "I am..." is very wrong. But when we get out of the " I am" state and unite, that is the REAL STATE OF US. Reaching that level of understanding is extremely difficult. We give more importance to self rather than the 'we' concept.

On Earth, we want money. Sunil has this much money, Poonam has this much, Renu has..., Papa has this much. Here money divides us all, but the inner state of SAMBHOG KAAYA has that energy that CLOUD has. That accumulates in emptiness, it has tremendous power in it. ***Collect the desire to EMPTY yourself for the COLLECTIVE benefit of others, instead of money. Then You can ask for anything out of Emptiness, Money, Peace, Happiness, health,*** pray for your children for their health and wellbeing. This all comes from that source, not from money.

So this state of emptiness is one thing that gives you that experience. We can understand how this world works, and also understand how money works. We understand the importance of cosmic energy which we collect inside Sambhog Kaaya. So it is necessary to understand meditation, emptiness, and Lotus Sutra which I have been talking about for the last 20 years, and hope that you realize its importance and you too benefit from it after reading it. I am trying to bring you to the level where you can understand, so all can benefit from it.

Awareness

After observing this body and creation. I have noticed three important things in my body which I can see, which everybody has.

1. God: Some individuals have few seeds or particles of God in them, and some have more. Those who have less of God's seeds in them, their awareness is less and those who have more of God's particles in them, their awareness is also more. Those who have higher awareness or have more God particles in them, they

possess that much greater personality, better health and more wealth.

2. Shadow of God: Image, Shadow, Mirror image, Maya, or Emptiness. These are the terms I use. As much as God's awareness is there, an individual must have that much God's shadow. When Gods of Plane 15 descended to 16th level for the purpose of creation, they created their own images and moved along with the images. At this stage the cosmic frequency of God and physical frequency of shadow of God were synchronized. This is how God / Atma and Shadow (Emptiness, Maya,) were perfectly balanced in the beginning. But as the time passed by, Gods with their shadows interacted with other Gods and their shadows, which created disturbance in their frequencies. This caused instability / severe disturbances and also in turn resulted in negative Karmas. Stable balance between atmas and their shadows got disturbed. The Maya factor increased far beyond that of atma. This imbalance between atmas and shadows increased a million fold as Gods along with their shadows moved further into lower planes with increased interactions with others. The situation turned very complex. They stagnated at lower planes. They could not rise to higher planes unless shadows were cleared from accumulated Karmas. This could be possible through the wisdom of Lotus Sutra which is the filtration system to purify the shadows to its original form. Once purified to their original status

these shadows along with their Gods/ Atmas could move to a higher plane which is their home.

"I ", Aham or Ego: Everyone has this. It has no identity of its own but everyone gives it a lot of weightage. The more we try to reduce the 'I", the more God's energy increases and the Maya tries to increase the ego. An effort is made that ego be the same for all. Ego properties have no identity but because of it a lot of exchange happens between all individuals.

If my ego is more, I am giving my Energies/ Shakti to others. If the person opposite me has a higher ego, then he is giving me his Shakti. This exchange between the two, has in itself, no identity. If the individual is intelligent, he understands that ego has no reality and thinks of himself as nothing but as shadow or Maya, and doesn't think of himself as God and does not react. Ego keeps reminding him that YOU EXIST. You are a CREATION of God, but by forgetting yourself, the opposite individual's Shakti, is taken up by you which enters your body and you show no reaction whatsoever. You remain calm. and you walk away. This observation makes you understand the knowledge of Lotus Sutra.

At every stage, be *reactionless, nothingness, emptiness,* and keep yourself in that state. The opposite person will always do something or other to you. Nature is also trying to do something to you.

For e.g. The flow of air in the mountains tries to move you to and fro and if you show fear then you have reacted negatively. If you get tuned in to its pleasantness, you have reacted positively. But if you have observed the air, the breeze surrounding you and it is nothing more to you than that. then it is nothing to you, no exchange took place. In this case, no exchange of energies takes place because air is nature's basic requirement.

While an Individual talks to you, every moment of it creates some reaction. When Parents or elders with love, or with fear try to advise you then they are giving you their energy or strength. If you accept their advice without reacting irrespective of whether you believe it or not, if you listen to it with peace then their energies come into you. *They will help you.* If you react negatively and think it is rubbish what they are saying, then you are at a loss because that Shakti turns negative inside you, and if you took the advice with respect and love then that Shakti which came inside you will stay with you in the way you felt it.

In this way, opposite individuals' energy comes as Karma to you, we call it SAMBHOG KAAYA. This will protect you or harm you. Because if the opposite person is giving you negative energy and is going to harm you, and if you react to it then his negativity gets collected inside you. Either you reap the actions or dissolve them with awareness.

Bhoot pret or ghost is an accumulated energy - concentrated accumulated energy because they have no body, so no outlet, no place to go, and as it has no wisdom that they can't clean themselves, they are in too much misery because of it. Then they try to get into some person's body, they go and pacify their sorrows or suffering to cool it down.

But all these ghosts can surround the BODY and are filled with misery. They try to enter only that person who remains in EMPTINESS and is reactionless. But that place is so small for them. Normally Bhoot/Pret cannot enter. Some special people who by meditation or awareness, can create a lot of VOID or EMPTINESS, then that becomes a problem for the ghost and not for normal individuals.

My Method Of Meditation

Our body and mind primarily consist of two major elements. One is the God element and the second is the creation element. The creation element came after God decided to have creation. And God produced an Image of himself. We can call that an Illusion, Mirage, Emptiness, or Shadow, a Mirror image.

These are the two basic elements from which this existence or creation started. Our body has these two basic elements. There are also two methods of meditation.

First method: To meditate on any one point in the body. Concentrate all the God energy on that one point and rise in your body through Chakras. One after the other seven Chakras in your body get formed due to the process of creation. That means you are going back on the path on which creation moved forward. So you go back to the top, Crown Chakra and then you go back to God, leaving behind the creation. This method is one basic method of meditation, which most of our saints in ancient India followed. Primarily there was no other method available initially. But God, understanding the limitation of creation, developed wisdom energy in its body which we called the Lotus Sutra.

The History of the development of the Lotus Sutra is given in a book that is available in the market. Lotus Sutra was initially spoken by Gautam Buddha when he was alive in physical life, 2560 years back. We can say, as per the history of Lotus Sutra, that it was born billions of years back but it was not available on Earth. It is due to the efforts of Buddhas in the lineage that Gautam Buddha was the one who visited our Earth and he is the one who brought down the Lotus Sutra.

Second Method: This is possible and successful and better than the first method of meditation, where one starts the journey from God and goes back to God, without helping the creation but the second method is better. With the help of the Lotus Sutra which came into existence because of Gautam Buddha on this Earth, that person can develop and help in the creation. That means he has to expand the creation from wherever it is, to a higher level. This process has been going on for billions of years since the Lotus Sutra was born. If you read the book on Lotus Sutra whose English translations are done by Burton Watson and others, you will find that Lotus Sutra was born billion-trillion years back in higher planes and it has been brought down slowly and slowly till it reached Earth with the help of Gautam Buddha. Without the wisdom of the Lotus Sutra, you can't help the creation go further.

In the series of ten Avatars, the ninth avatar is Buddha and without Buddha bringing down Lotus Sutra you cannot help the creation enhance further. So it is very necessary that the second method of meditation has to follow a Lotus Sutra Wisdom. **Now, what is the second method of meditation?**

The God element remains in you and it has to go back to God, whether you go back to God through the second method of meditation or the traditional method of meditation or you do not do it doesn't matter, because ultimately the God element will go to God at the end of Maha Pralaya or after a lapse. And that doesn't require the first method of meditation., The first method of meditation is like running away from the situation God has brought you to.

Since the Lotus Sutra is available on Earth the second method has to be followed in meditation and that is the meditation I do. My meditation is on creation and creation is 99% in my body. The God element is at the back which I know through the energy in my body.

That means in my body I can feel God by just being AWARE. If I am aware then that means the God in me is aware. He is always with me. He will always be with me. Millions of elements in my body that are divided as part of creation are the ones that are to be adjusted, moved in my body through the awareness of God, and continuously made into a better creation.

Now, what is the purpose of my Second method of meditation, which I do with the help of the Lotus Sutra? It is to improve my body. My body should be so good that all the creations around me should be easily available to me. My mind should be so sharp that I can conceive any profitable situation thereby increasing my world's facilities and amenities. My Body Wisdom should be such that I should be able to enjoy the prosperity and luxuries that I create around me happily enjoying it. That means my health is so perfect that it doesn't bypass or move me away from the happiness of creating luxuries. So the second point is that my creation should improve to that level with the wisdom of the Lotus Sutra that my health is perfect and due to perfect health, I can enjoy the luxuries around me. Third thing is that my body should age slowly compared to the natural surroundings. If other people start becoming old at the age of 80s or 90s, I should feel younger than them at that age. That means my creation has to be much advanced so that I can enjoy the luxuries of life/ creation for a longer period.

The next important factor is a reduced old age, despite enjoying the luxuries of life with better health. I am peaceful because, in my development of wisdom, I understand that enjoyment brings variation. Sometimes it is more enjoyable, sometimes it is less enjoyable and this variation also causes unhappiness. But if I am peaceful and balanced, whether that situation is enjoyable or not then these variations will not affect me.

So my method should give me the following results. My method of meditation with the help of the Lotus Sutra which is brought down by Buddhas should give me the following benefits:

First, it should bring me down to a level where my existence becomes struggle free. And later when I am developed or evolved, it should bring even some *luxuries,* better than the average person. Then it should bring better *health* than the average person. And then it should bring *peace* better than the average level. If that is the way I am following my meditation then that's the method of meditation of creation. This process of meditation on creation is extremely interesting and Lotus Sutra gives many hints when you walk on this path.

The evolution has also created ten levels of Avatars, which means the evolution has moved forward. Because we in our limited awareness are not able to take the help of Lotus Sutra to move the creation further then God comes down on Earth, takes a specific body which is suitable for it and he comes with the wisdom of Lotus Sutra and then evolves further, and tries to push the creation to a higher level. That person after becoming a Buddha becomes a Kalki. So Kalki is an Ultimate tool. A person who is a Kalki is supposed to have two very important things in his body.

One is the God element in the highest form which means deepest awareness and second is the wisdom of the Lotus Sutra.

The Action, Progress & Process Of Chakras In My Body.

The Nabhi Chakra / Solar Plexus or Manipura, which is the third Chakra from the bottom, which acts as the body's energy powerhouse and from where the ghost enters and dwells, is little above it. All of us are born on Earth at Navel level.

So we start from the bottom of the Spine. The bottom or Root Chakra is termed as Muladhara Chakra. The second is Sacral Chakra, Swadhisthana. The third mentioned is Manipura, which is a little above the Navel, and generates a lot of heat. The next chakra, the fourth, is Heart Chakra, also called Anahata. The fifth is Throat Chakra- Vishuddha Chakra. The sixth is Ajna Chakra- the third eye and the seventh is Crown Chakra or Sahasrara Chakra.

In my meditation when I was handling ghosts, I was sometimes at a lower level or Muladhara and mostly at

Navel level where a child is born, connected with Mother.

After I died in my 80s when I was given extensive protection, my Chakra energy started rising beyond the Navel Chakra, and it was a very painful process.

In between the Heart Chakra and Navel, there is a Chakra, Manipura, which generates a lot of heat. When my body energy would rise from there, I would feel extreme pain in the stomach and my whole body would get heated . I would start perspiring instantly because of the heat. This process became very intense because I was not able to penetrate that Chakra and my meditation insisted on rising above so it had to go through that penetration and I became unconscious many times because of extreme pain. This happened four-five times.

Now I have almost crossed that and sometimes I touch my Heart Chakra. Normally I remain at Nabhi, which is a little below Manipura Chakra because I want to work at Nabhi Chakra, the source where 'I' originated. ***Muladhara Chakra attracts me because of ghosts.*** My work there is almost finished. Not that all the ghosts have been cleansed but now I have stopped that work because I have done my maximum there.

Earth level Chakra will remain active till I am alive in this life. The Navel Chakra will remain alive. Mostly I will remain in my Nabhi energy, till I am in this life.

When I meditate in the morning or at midnight, my energy starts rising and it penetrates and reaches Heart Chakra and this process will continue. It passes so fast through my Throat Chakra, through forehead Chakra, and my Crown Chakra. As soon as the heat and pain is generated in the Heart Chakra energy penetrates and rushes to the Crown. It hardly takes any time. I immediately understand, that now the pain will be gone, the heat will be gone because *that blockage at that Chakra is no more.* This process of Chakras is at present going on in my body. With continued meditation, energy is expected to rise above Heart Chakra to create a higher level of emptiness.

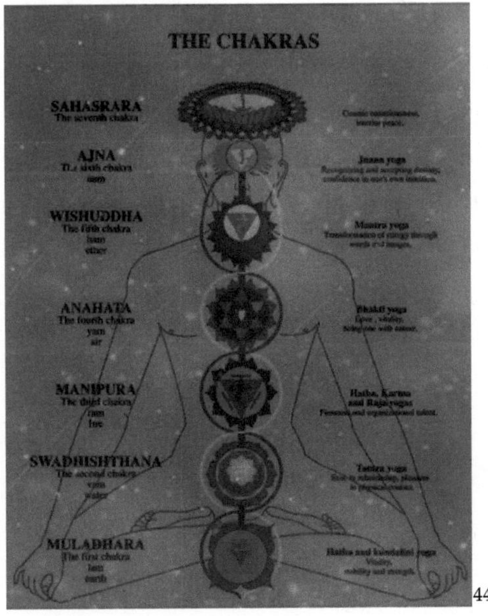

[44]

44 Courtesy: https://in.pinterest.com/pin/426223552247253835/

I don't have to reach Crown Chakra. It is not my purpose. It is not even my purpose to rise above my Navel point. I will rise from the Navel point without meditation, that is going to happen. Energy arising has risen in a huge quantity from my Muladhara chakra or high energy has been generated from there and now when it will start generating Earth energy it will start affecting surroundings and people on Earth. In between, Muladhara Chakra becomes active because there are many souls in the ghost level who are of a high level of existence but they are passing through Hell. So while passing through Hell, if they enter my body then I along with that soul go through that Muladhara Chakra process. Then we both go together to Higher levels and then we go very fast.

The Navel / Nabhi Chakra is particularly connected with the etheric plane, which is concerned with the distribution of energy. This Chakra helps to coordinate the movement of energy in the body through the Nadis.

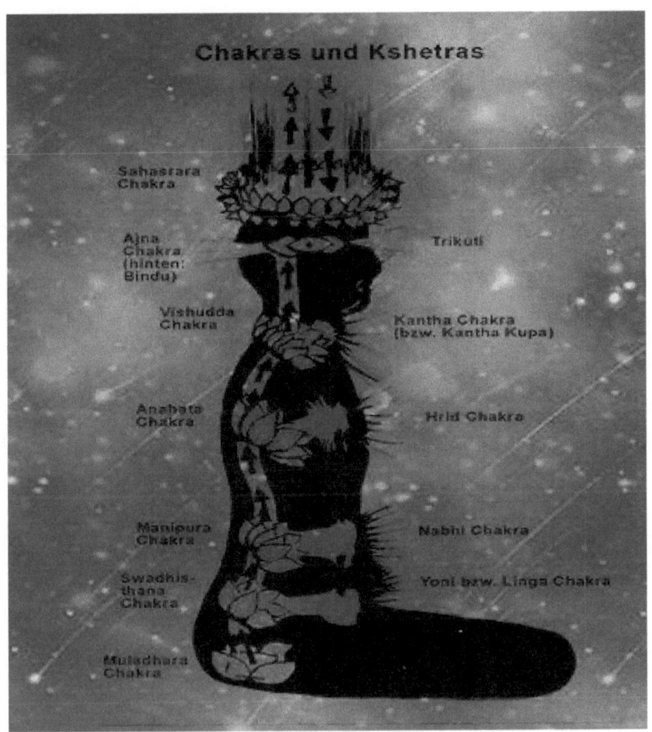

Rising through Chakras[45] is very complex and time consuming process in lower planes such as in our plane. Here, Lokas are overcrowded and thus cleansing process through Chakras will take many years, beyond the life span of human beings, but that process of Cleaning of Earth or rising above my Nabhi point will continue even after my death, through my meditation process connected with Lotus Sutra. .

Sometimes I meet certain people, who are very good at looking in your astral body. There is a lady who lives

45 Courtesy: https://in.pinterest.com/pin/510595676517459870/

near my house, who got solely attracted to me because of my Chakras. She deliberately tried to befriend us and asked me certain questions and ultimately she said, *"Your Chakras are working at Muladhara Chakra and there is a lot of commotion there"*. I brought her to my house because she was quite persuasive but later on we told her, that we are not interested in Chakra System and my energy will mostly remain at Muladhara and Nabhi chakras because I do not have any interest in raising my energies to higher levels and if she finds commotion, there is a purpose behind it and if she observes that there is a lot of whirling and swirling in those areas, I told her not to *bother about it. That was my system of meditation.*

Even though I would meet many people who used to talk about the Chakras in my body, I would not bother, because *I knew my process starts from Nabhi, collects energies from up and down Chakras, and creates a DharmaKaya, Nirmaan Kaaya & Sambhog Kaaya of my body*. I could make that energy rise through the Crown but as mentioned in Lotus Sutra in the very first Chapter, it very clearly mentions that *Energy does Nothing*, and I have listened clearly in my meditation that energy which goes above the Crown takes the person to Source from where he started his journey, that is, towards God. It definitely brings Moksh to that person. But elements in its body remain as they are, and again, another form of God/ Soul comes in and occupies that seed body, and the same person arises. I was not interested in that. What I am interested in is the seed in my body which started at the Nabhi circle and Collected energies from around it and expanded. That's my process.

Many individuals visualize and practice the Muladhara to Crown chakra meditation i.e. vertically rising, and if they focus on the navel chakra, few of them can see horizontal lines entering the Navel and that cords are tied/closed, meaning not to enter the world or that portal. There are many other Healing techniques like Theta Healing, Pranic Healing & Reiki Healing which teach us to heal our body.

These healing processes bring awareness and are somewhat similar to OBSERVING AND DISSOLVING.

Let me continue with my process. When the ghost enters, it enters through my two lower chakras.

I have not read about Chakras in Buddhism. Even the Vipassana or Metta meditation is done on the outer surface of the body. First three days the meditation is done to increase concentration and awareness. *This is done by observing the breathing.*

I dissolve pain by inviting its full force and observing this pain with awareness. The same method that I used on arising painful energies from Muladhara Chakra due to ghost's entry.

In introspection I believe that I broke that cord in 1994, which many individuals do not dare to tread when I requested Narayana 3 times, and then I was handed over to Buddhas.

One more thing I have observed is that energies, ghosts, and Spirits entering my body are on some days more and some days less. I tried keeping a monthly chart to check whether the miserable energies were more prevalent as per the lunar cycle, i.e., worse during 'no moon' or other days. But it was not so.

Finally, I concluded that if I went to crowded places, like some marriage functions or Ganesh Chaturthi at home, I would be very uneasy. And my sleep that day would be very painful till I cleared the energies through Awareness. Also, by the end of the day, these energies get accumulated and need to be cleaned. It also depends on the locality I am staying in and the vibes/energies I collect over the day.

Incident, when my Energy suddenly rose in The presence of my family:

I became unconscious when my energy suddenly rose in the presence of my Family. This incident happened some six months back, in the presence of my wife and my two grandsons, Ish & Raj. Their parents had gone away for some function, and Ish and Raj were with us. It was mutual taking care of each other. We all four felt like having a little Outing and enjoying ourselves. So my grandson suggested that we play golf from 12 noon till 12:30 pm and then later enjoy a five-star meal at a restaurant.

So my wife, my two grandsons and I went to Sentosa Hotel. We sat there, naturally, I liked beer & fish, and my grandchildren liked a lot of non-veg stuff. Everything was ordered, but I knew I should take very light food. So for the final meal, I ordered only Daal and Rice. My grandchildren ate whatever they liked.

When the meal was almost finished, I was probably in extreme happiness that my grandchildren are as much connected with me as my son and my daughters. Out of that feeling of happiness of sharing a rare moment with my grandchildren where we all four of us were re-living as children and happy, I do not know what happened, suddenly my energy started rising from Nabhi level to Heart Chakra. It rose so forcefully that I was taking a scoop of rice and Daal to my mouth and I suddenly felt a strong pain. I silently kept the spoon down and then I do not know what happened.

After about ten minutes my wife says *ten minutes*, but I do not think it was ten minutes because certain actions had happened in my absence, that may be five minutes or so.

As described by my grandchildren and my wife, I will tell you what they said. My wife said that she saw *my eyes moving up and down and something coming out of my mouth.* So she rose, and she cleaned that. My Grandchildren thought that I had a serious stroke and I had gone from this life. The waiters around me were so panicky that they moved away, leaving us four at our table alone.

Naturally, Ish (the elder one) took over the responsibility. His nature is quiet and calm. Raj did not know what to do. Ish rose and went to pay the bill. It must have taken five minutes. My wife says ten minutes. So whatever it is. By the time the bill was cleared, he was thinking of the next step, and I suddenly came back to my normal self. I knew something had happened, and I had missed it. I felt completely okay because the energy had penetrated the whole of my body. The pain was gone, and the Crown Chakra and my Eye Chakra were quite alive, so I knew I had now become normal. I have gone through this kind of process a few times in the past. So I understood it. So I said to my grandson, *"What has happened? Why have you cleared the bill? What about completing the little food that is left on my plate?"*

They were also perplexed and surprised, and they couldn't understand what was happening. They wondered, *'Dada (me) was almost dead and suddenly talking as if everything was normal.'*

But it was a shocking experience for them. They wanted to leave that place and said, *"Chalo Dada, Chalo Utho."* They caught me by my shoulder. I said, *"Why? I am ok now."* They didn't listen to me. They guided me to the car and took me home and the doctor was called and everything was found to be normal. This has happened in the presence of my immediate family.

Chapter 9

"Because the Buddha has emitted this ray of light,[46]
I and those with me in the assembly can see
these worlds of marvellous and varied beauty.
The wisdom and transcendent powers of all the Buddhas are extraordinary;
By emitting a single ray of light He has illuminated innumerable lands"

~ **Lotus Sutra**

The Shining Star

Looking back and reflecting on my life, I consider the event of Star that entered my body in 1951 in Delhi while sleeping on the cot under the sky was a God of Awareness from between 0 to 15 planes. This means this was not a Star but a Son of God who had entered my body in 1951.

Post that day my whole life was being guided by this Star. I did not know that the communication I received all my life was from this Star which was working in my body. As I had mentioned earlier, I was inspired by the status attained by my maternal uncle in the society. He

---

46 Ray of Light in between Buddha's eyebrows

(ref LS pg 6 and 15 in Appendix pg xxxii and xxxiv resp.)

was well qualified and impressed people by his talks on meditation and other spiritual subjects. However his way of meditation took him towards a wrong path and he became self centered and ruined his family life by going in for a second marriage. Extent of disruption in the family was a shocking experience for me and this incident became a major point in deciding my future method of meditation and spirituality.

The same Star guided me to Tirupati, which I talk about later on so I should understand that there are powers that are beyond this physical life and they have to be accepted and experienced. The same Star made my life uncomfortable, in the sense by the age of 50, I was restless at that time though I had earned a good living I earned bad health.

Ultimately that made my life miserable. This misery created questions in my mind about the purpose of life, the purpose of creation, etc. I was unaware that the same Star led me to Vipassana meditation at Igadpuri in 1992 but after that, things changed. For the first time on 30th June 1992, direct communication between that Star and me, the experience which I have mentioned in the visibility of my Body Karmas earlier was giving me a feeling that there is something inside me that is trying to communicate. This was the first incident, where I understood that *some power is guiding me*. The Voice or the force of that power was so strong that the communication became clear after that, and every moment of my life was then under the control of the Star.

It made me look at my body and the formation of Karmas. Awareness made me clear of those karmas and re-form them to the right pattern whereby I could get good health back. This was the initial benefit I got by doing Vipassana meditation in the form in which my inner Star guided me and made me believe to keep the connection strong. Next two years, for 12 hours a day, day and night I kept in contact with that Star. I was so fascinated with this Star and the power of awareness in my body which was bringing in many changes. Looking at awareness in the body with the power of the Star I was able to understand EMPTINESS, which I saw in my body when vibrations and sensations disappeared from my body. Slowly this emptiness that was widening in my body in the next two years of my meditation made me sure enough that I am on the right path. Prior to this, this Star was the reason for my contact with Tirupati God whose name is Narayana. Later on when I asked the questions they were still not answered., the main question was, "WHAT IS THE PURPOSE OF LIFE".

The same star in 1994, led me to ask for a boon in the form of my becoming a Buddha. At this point, without knowing the Ten Avatars I had asked my role to change from Krishna to Buddha and the same Star must have led me deliberately but slowly to this answer. The same Star later brought me in contact with

Lotus Sutra because the Wisdom that I was pouring in, gave me the answers which were coming from that same Star, were in concurrence with Lotus Sutra. This is how it made me look at and search for this Lotus Sutra that was spoken by Gautam Buddha whose details I have been giving many times in this book.

When I started studying the Lotus Sutra book along with my meditation, everything started becoming clear. In fact, just by meditating on the Lotus Sutra, the Star was leading me to two important powers. My emptiness in my body was making outer world energy surrounding me enter my body and create sensations and clearing them would create wisdom in my body. Plus those outside energies such as ghosts or Spirits entering my body which were cleansed and transformed into emptiness was increasing my power. In other words, my process was becoming more powerful. As if my body was getting more energetic and I was able to create the emptiness faster and also process the energies entering from outside faster.

The same Star led me to an experience with that Ghost Master in North India and gave me the first experience of the Dark Powers that exist in Hell. The same Star guided me when that Ghost Master started using powers on me and this process of facing the ghost in my body made me aware of my powers and that I could handle any ghost with any power. The Ghost Master was not an ordinary ghost, *he was a Pisach - a very powerful Human Body that existed on earth and in lower lokas*. Later on, I came to know that he had a sister in the ghost world who was leading a large number of ghosts because the same ghost attacked me, day and night for the next fifteen years but this process was required and I am sure my Star deliberately led me to that Evil world of Hell, where million of Ghost were to be encountered.

Later on, I came to understand that all this has been done to me by the Star to change my body in the *first stage from Krishna to Buddha and in the second stage from Buddha to Kalki*. Let us understand this transformation from Krishna to Kalki.

In the first stage when I was creating *emptiness* and expanding my body by bringing in the outer energies, I was doing the work of Buddha because every cosmic energy that was entering my body was evil energy that caused suffering to others, and the atmosphere around me was filled with those evil energies emitted by many souls. These evil energies would cause pain and suffering in my body and the Star of awareness would filter or clear that evilness and cause emptiness. The process itself led my body to develop wisdom and later on I learned the world of *Jhanas*. Each evil energy that was entering my body was of a different nature as well as of a different intensity and each one of them required a different type of wisdom to deal with it. So my body in the next 15 years was collecting all sorts of negative, evil energies of variable intensities and developing Jhanas many in number.

These Jhanas are like pearls woven on a string and they form the Lotus Sutra. So in fact I was led to install Lotus Sutra in my body with the help of the Star. This process of development of Lotus Sutra and expansion of my body to receive much more energy at every step is the process that a Kalki has to know. This is why I was transferring my body slowly from Buddha to Kalkiness.

Human Analogy From The Womb

A person is born in his mother's womb, and his body and mind develop slowly and change. This is similar to the analogy of Indian Avatars. In the mother's womb, firstly, he looks like a form of seed, which converts to *fish* within a few days, and after that, it looks like a *tortoise* in 3 to 5 days. In three months, he will develop into a *Bauna* with a large head and tail, which looks like a *Narsimha avata*r or a Lion face animal. That means it is said that these four avatars, i.e., fish, tortoise, boar, and Narsimha, the lion shape, come up in a mother's womb before he comes out in the fifth/ sixth stage as a human being-Parashuram.

He, the emotional child, grows and learns to control his emotions, and then after learning, earning, and maintaining a family, he behaves like Shri Ram. Some of us stop our growth after reaching the level of *Ram.* But some others start their own business or occupy high positions in a company where they control many people and businesses. They are the ones who decide the fate of lots of people. These become *Krishna*. The next level of Krishna is *Buddha* and then finally *Kalki*.

So, this evolution process and my story from birth to death look similar. I went through the phase of Shri Ram between 1959 and 1971 while I looked after my family. Between 1972 to 1994, I entered the phase of Krishna. I had established my own factory and had many employees under me. I didn't stop at that level, but I went on searching for the Truth. Up to the age of 50, Narayana helped me grow from a child to Ram and then to Krishna, and when I crossed 55 years of age, he handed me over to Buddha. That means I started walking on the path of Buddha at the age of around 57 years. At 57 years , I was trying to become Kalki with the help of Buddha.

Now, What is Kalki? Kalki is shown to be riding on a horse with a sword. He comes at the end of this era to finish all the evil energies, to eliminate total Evilness.

Does that mean, that if a person rides a Horse and starts killing evil people with his Sword, he is known as Kalki? No, it is not that. Kalki is a highly evolved Avatar who would enter the evil zone and destroy all the evilness. He rides a Flying Horse and Sword in his hand to pave the way toward the beginning of Satyug.

When I was 57 years old, I felt I had entered the stage to become Kalki. It was like acquiring a Winged Horse and Sword, empowered by Lotus Sutra to travel inside the body. It can enable you to travel anywhere in the Universe.

It can be compared to a Horse with Wings on which Kalki is riding. The Horse with Wings is evolving or developing, and Kalki, who is controlling it and riding on it, must go to the higher evolution. Precisely this is what happened to me. That means when I was around 60 years, I came across literature, which led me to Lotus Sutra. A holy literature of Gautam Buddha. It is like finding a *rusted Sword* that had not been used for billions of years in the form of the Lotus Sutra.

A rusted Sword was given to Kalki, who was riding on a winged horse. He starts entering the evil empire of ghosts and evil persons, annihilating them and starts extracting evil juice out of them, converting them into something pure. It is like increasing the power of the Horse, increasing the power of its Wings so that it can fly higher and penetrate into deeper regions. Also, the shining of the sword signifies that it can become sharper and eradicate evil to a greater extent.

https://in.pinterest.com/pin/17381148546420404/

Later on, when I died at 80, my sword and wings were not that strong. I died because of my weakness in the sea of evilness, where I was also severely hurt.

But here comes a vision of my death at the age of 80. It showed a mistake in the creation, and that growth to Kalkihood should have been systematic and error-free but was not. And the leader who came into my vision was a person who controlled both the worlds of Buddha & Gods. He admitted the mistake that I was not given Zero level protection. I had been given fifth-level protection- that means I should not have been allowed to enter the extreme evil place because my horse was not strong enough, and my sword was not sharp enough to face the situation. That mistake was rectified at 80, and I have continued my mission since then. I still go down to Hell fighting with evil and keep strengthening my horse, wings, and sword.

After 83 - 84 years, I was told that my sword and horse would get more robust in this era. With these weapons available to you, you can eradicate as much evilness as you can, and the rest of the evils which will remain in the creation will be destroyed in the next Era. This summarizes my life and has been the purpose of my life.

Different Stages Of Avatar

The life of Ram Peswani after this incident when the Star entered his body was totally controlled by the Star. The communication was only one way. Ram Peswani was ignorant and Star had a very powerful mind so it was very easy to control the mind of Ram Peswani and direct him to evolve correctly.

All incidents in the life of Ram Peswani after that are guided and led by Star or Kalki. His association with his Uncle, his visit to Tirupati, his sickness, and illnesses which made him leave this world with warning. All incidents were led by this one powerful mind, till at the age of 55 for the first time on 30th June 1995 the Communication became two way. For the first time on that day, Ram Peswani came to know that Voice who was controlling all his life and felt happy to be connected to that Voice. This communication which had improved after 1994 strengthened. During the period of 1992-94, Lotus Sutra which existed in the body of Ram Peswani can be described as a Sword rusted from millions of years ago from previous Era. It was dirty and sort of in an unshapely condition, lying in the body of Ram Peswani. It was brought out in 1992 and was cleaned and polished for two years up to 1994. This is the process which is described as the cleaning of the body of Ram Peswani, so that communication can be very easy and totally powerful and nothing can disconnect it. This communication between the Star & the most important point of the Star, the weapon which is the hands of Ram Peswani. Here the Star gets the body of Ram Peswani to synchronize with himself, which is like a Horse & the Sword also which Ram Peswani has been brought out and polished & cleaned.

After 1994 it was very important that Ram Peswani along with Star should be able to use this Sword so that it can extend its powers or its range and also help to clean plane no. 26 in a better way. For this, page 65 of Lotus Sutra(by Burton Watson), describes Pishacha Demons, who are the most advanced Demons, who are a higher form of Ghost who use part goodness to evolve to a higher level and create havoc in existence. So it was very important for Ram Peswani to meet these Pisach[4] Demons and hence the life and experience led him to that Guru who was Ghost Master on Earth. The details of which I have given. All the thirty years of my experience of facing ghosts or demons and Pisach Demons and also of one of my daughter's experiences can be a detailed topic in itself.

A little bit of evolution of the Pishacha demon is necessary. These Pishacha Demons are very intelligent. They knew how to advance with some part of goodness that they have in them and they also knew the art of leading with fear. Small souls get captured by him and Pishacha makes them do his dirty work. So this Pishacha / Demon Master who Ram Peswani faced had a sister in the world of ghosts. The evolution in the world of Ghosts is like Ants & Bees. This sister had many Ghosts under her control who could not exist without her. They were devoted to that Sister ghost of this Demon Master. The demon Master controlled the Sister and the Sister controlled the Ghosts.

Ram Peswani in his body along with the Star power had to go through all of them in the next fifteen years and this was the period when his Sword was Shining, getting brighter and extending. But in that experience, his body had to go through a lot of pain which has been described.

Present Stage Of Avatar

He is now totally ready, perfect with his body or horse, i.e.Ram Peswani is one with him. His Sword is Shining and bright. It has a whole combination of Kalki, the Star son, the body of the horse, and the sword of Lotus Sutra are all one. They are all together. They are not separate now and the work of cleaning this Earth is going on at speed. It is expected that this Kalki with the body of horse and sword will do his work perfectly in the coming years and he will be capable of doing an enormous transformation on this Earth. The body of Ram Peswani itself will also face the effects of this work and growth will be seen in the form of prosperity, peace, happiness, unity with his relatives, friends and neighbors, and love around because that is the core of Lotus Sutra or Kalki.

Chapter 10

"A Buddha is a child, and the Lotus Sutra is its parent.
If the parents of thousand children are praised,
those thousand children will rejoice."[47]

A Message To My Children & Grandchildren

My nine grandchildren, one great-grandchild and my future generations, a message to you all. Be torch-bearers for all lost souls. Never try to hurt or harm anyone. This book may seem a little far-fetched to you all but you might connect with this easily if you have seen the Marvel Series- Avengers. or the movie Avatar, Indian movie Raaz 3 etc.

The whole series of Avengers talks about Infinity stones. The Infinity Stones are a group of gems that grant their owner great powers. *These powers get into the head of the person that holds it. Thanos got hold of this Infinity Stone.* Each stone represents a different aspect of the Universe (Space, Mind, Reality, Power, Time, and Soul).

Infinity Stones are really powerful gems that, when united, can be used to destroy people, planets, solar systems—you name it.

---

47 Courtesy : https://www.nichirenlibrary.org/en/wnd-1/Content/127#p949

Thanos believes that if he kills half of all life in the Universe, he'll restore balance. To do so, he needs all six Infinity Stones to power his Infinity Gauntlet, which in turn would give him the ability to bend time, space, energy, and the laws of physics and reality.

Thanos' actions harm Earth's political, economic, and social stability. Who knows how much turmoil the snap and the subsequent blip caused on countless alien worlds?

Even in Avatar, there's a scene where small, glowing seeds from the tree of souls descend upon and encompass Jake that seems like a reference to the anointing of the Holy Spirit. The idea of the Na'vi's ability to Connect to the spiritual world physically is an interesting and novel experience to connect with the Divine and the reality of mass prayer. Nature is infused with her divine Spirit. Sully learns that the Na'vi practices forms of telepathy and sacred bonding with both fellow Navi and phantasmagoric animals. A Na'vi tells the increasingly wide-eyed ex-marine that there is a "flow of energy" that inhabits everything.

It should be easy to explain Lotus Sutra to my children and grandchildren. They understand and recognize the misuse of occult powers in hands of so-called Masters (like Thanos) having their point of views, and also that nature is infused with Divine Spirit. Through movies, they relate to issues we otherwise find hard to explain to them.

Just because we are focusing on newer technologies and science, doesn't mean such mystic things do not occur. Even ISRO makes sure to execute or launch their projects during auspicious times or Shubh Mahurats.

The Science we read and practice is only Material Science. It doesn't accept or deny other dimensions of science, e.g. paranormal, because it is different, and the laws of Material Science do not apply here. Science fails to explain anything which is beyond matter (or convertible energy as per Einstein's equation).

Can Science explain what Consciousness is? Can Science explain what a Dream is? How do people experience phenomena like Deja vu[48]? The more you learn, the more you realize that there is lots more that is unknown and more questions arise. As you advance in spirituality, you begin to realize that spiritual laws are at work and that you and your knowledge are a mere drop in the vast ocean .

Therefore I would advise you not to use Science to deny things that are unexplained. A lot more is yet to be discovered.

Issac Newton had once said that he felt like a boy playing on the sea shore, throwing pebbles in the sea,

---

48 déjà vu, which means "already seen" in French.

Couresy:https://www.sciencealert.com/the-mysterious-phenomenon-of-dj-vu-is-finally-closer-to-being-explained whilst the great ocean of truth lay all undiscovered before him.

If your heart is pure and your soul powerful, you can defeat any evil in this world. Please honor your time, and your life and never go against your conscience or soul.

If your mind is weak, you may fail to judge the real intentions behind their fake outward behaviors. They may be your closest relatives, friends, or neighbors, who hold a special place in your heart. They might have given you body, mind, and time, and you feel obliged to make them happy. Outwardly though he/she may show concern for you and your family, but internally holds envy, a grudge because of some family arguments, and also because you have everything that he/she yearns for. Outwardly they may project themselves as your well-wishers by guiding you on the right path, but internally, using the help of Ghost Masters, they manipulate and destroy your family unity by penetrating the dark forces inside and controlling your mind.

You should be AWARE of these so called relatives. These so-called relatives and friends are a ***burden*** to society and on Earth and harm themselves more than others. They bring the worst behavior out of you and make you feel you are right by your wrong reasoning. Your family is your strength. In your bad times, your so-called girlfriend/boyfriend, money, and success, everything may leave you, but your family / spouse will always be there.

Love your family more than you love your possessions, money, career, or hobbies. That other stuff can't love you back. Everything in life has an end but love is eternal. *Sit still in awareness to reason out things in favor of Dharma.*

Buddham Sharnam Gacchami,

Sangam Sharnam Gachaami,

Dhamam Sharna Gacchami.

Some people mostly influence and attack the mind of a gullible person mainly to have sole control of his /her property and money and to make him a slave to their commands. They chose the head of the family so that they can influence and hold a place in his / her heart. Less people or no people will visit the person and the person too might not be going out anymore.

Nowadays, many people try to manipulate or control your destiny. These people succumb to these Ghost Masters to get all the pleasures, riches, and wealth in life, once they know the easy way to earn respect, power, and money they cannot resist continuing to manipulate through Dark Forces whatever they want in life and their surroundings and neighbors. They will cheat their friends without hesitation or dump their religious or moral codes when the stakes become high. Sometimes they get from their Ghost Masters, water filled with prayers, and when they make others drink that water, whatever they wish for from that person, is done or comes true. Sometimes they use hair, magical prayers, animal sacrifices, nails, blood, or dust from your feet to facilitate the Demon's work. Then they try to balance their Karmas by making donations, showing off how generous they are.

The family that gets affected has to keep quiet and although they know something is not right, they cannot fight openly with these horrible people. They never know when these people will stab them by burning their effigies and destroy their family's health and peace of mind. There may be mysterious deaths in their family without any health problems. They can obtain the ultimate solution from the Prayers or a Guru or a person who knows and abides by LOTUS SUTRA.

Kalyug has many people who fall for lust, easy money, and power. Once they get all the luxuries you can give them, they start giving some excuses for being busy with their work and avoid you.. They keep collecting bad Karmas and when it is time for them to leave Earth they think they have control. But GOD is the ultimate judge.

Once people start using these ghosts they find it difficult to stop. If they stop they will incur great losses. So they continue to use the ghosts and indulge in bad deeds which result in accumulation of bad Karmas.

Such people who make use of ghosts can get fame, wealth and pleasure in life but it will be short lived. Majority of such people lose everything including family and become homeless. How can you make a deal with the Devil? He is a Master of lies, you gain a coin and he takes all your life. Don't sell your Soul to the Devil. This creature will promise you the world. Anything you want. But eternity is a lot longer than this life. Besides, your Soul is not yours to sell in the first place.

When you think, *"I'll sell my Soul to the Devil"*, then Dark Forces listen. It's hard because it seems like you could have a great life while you're alive if you sell your Soul. But a great life here for the next 100 years is like an hour of greatness compared to an eternity of misery. Eternity = time is not linear, so you will suffer indefinitely. You become all the pain you have ever felt and ever caused anyone else plus physical, emotional, and mental torture. And let's say you decide to get away from the association of ghosts, you may find it difficult as these ghosts try their best not to let you go. The curses and misery of the family you affected, makes you go through endless miseries with no respite.

But, your Soul belongs to God. It isn't yours to sell. However, God gave us all free will to make the decision to give our Souls to whoever we want to. If anyone reading this is smart, they won't even consider it, this is the wrong way to live life.

Life is like a stage for us to act in different roles at different moments. The best role is to be yourself, remaining positive and happy and having a heart to be grateful for whatever that you receive. We can share our happiness and wisdom with people who are lacking love and comfort.

Also, my son Sunil, expressed certain doubts that he had after reading this manuscript.

1. How did his sister, Gita- the mother of her two children Karan & Priya give them divine guidance and messages, after her death?

She died before completing her duties on Earth at the age of 38 years when her son was in 11th grade and daughter in 8th grade.

2. Question arises here as how are the messages given to them by their mother? If her soul has just been released now by Papa after 15-17 years of her death, how could she have guided them till now and be their Guardian Angel?

So I am including the meaning of TIME.

TIME holds absolutely no meaning after Death. IT IS RELATIVE.

It turns out that everything we see and experience is a whirl of information occurring in our heads. We are not just objects embedded in some external matrix ticking away 'out there'. Rather, Space and Time are the tools our mind uses to put it all together.

Also you only send part of your energy to incarnate into a physical vessel, the bigger part of you (or higher self) is always in the non-physical realm.

We have 3 bodies[49]

1. Physical Body - made out of earthly elements.

2. Astral Body -. It relates to our senses of feeling pleasure or pain.

3. Causal Body - It is a seed body which contains all our previous experiences, memories, habits and information on all our lives.

When the physical body dies, the Astral body and the Causal body remain together and visit loved ones to guide them from time to time. This happens throughout our lives as there is no time in the other realm and *all lives can be accessed simultaneously.* It is hard for us to comprehend because whilst we are living in this body we see ourselves as a separate entity or as an individual but this is not the truth. This is just a vessel and our true self is pure consciousness, pure energy and is limitless.

As you're reading this, you're experiencing a 'Now'. But consider: from your great-grandmother's perspective, your nows exist in her future and her great-grandmother's nows exist in her past. The words 'past' and 'future' are just ideas RELATIVE to each individual observer.

---

49 Courtesy : THE THREE BODIES AND FIVE SHEATHS

So what happened to your great-grandmother after she died? To start with - since time doesn't exist - there is no 'after death', except the death of her physical body.

Life may actually flash before our eyes as we die. Gitu, too, got a glimpse of time with loved ones and other happy memories. Also, the future of her children for whom she had the desire to be there for, she saw ahead their beautiful and sad moments. All the important events ahead where she could have been there for them to Protect and Guide them through life, to sail them across the storms of their lives, she had quick visions of those special moments too. Also after a few seconds glimpse, she immediately got stuck in the Demon Master's Hell eternally. Gitu was only released after I managed to subdue and release the hungry souls who kept her captive.

She is now her children's Personal Guardian Angel, ever ready to protect them and guide them.

Value Of Prayers Among Children

If a person does not pray or meditate, some Spirit can harm him when his mind becomes weak. Due to the constant overload of Karmas in the body, Spirits can easily enter and take control of his weak mind.

Therefore to save himself from such a situation, he must have a powerful Guru who gives him protection. Likewise, through the practice of awareness by meditation, his energies do not get wasted on emotions; rather, he saves those energies to empty his body of the unnecessary emotional energies and burdens. Thereby he fills it with pure Wisdom, which will protect him from Spirits. He will have more clarity in his life.

Heaven and Hell are not places you go to but how you relate with your world. So, take time in your daily schedule to talk to God, and request Him to guide you. Listen to your Inner Voice. Be alone and speculate. You may find many strange things for which you do not have answers, but if you reason out with awareness or pray or talk to God, you will be guided in the right direction. Divine guidance helps. Sometimes you have to dig deep and look beyond the obvious for solutions. Prevention is better than cure, especially in this dark age where you cannot trust anyone.

Prayer for the Protection of Family

Lord, I pray Your emotional, physical, and Spiritual protection over my kids (grandkids). Keep evil far from them, and help them to trust You as their refuge and strength. I pray You will guard their minds from harmful instruction, and grant them discernment to recognize the truth. I pray You will make them strong and courageous in the presence of danger, recognizing that You have overcome and will set right all injustice and wrong one day. Help them to find rest in Your shadow, as they live in the Spiritual shelter You provide for them. Let them know that the only safe place is in God and that their home on Earth is only temporary. -by Rebecca Jordan[50]

---

50 Courtesy : Author - *Rebecca Jordan*

We may not realize it but, ultimately, our past Karmas too, play a role in it. All this transient happiness and sadness drama revolves around our desires. Till the time there are desires we can not escape from sorrows. When one gets past one's desires then one feels no happiness or sadness, there remains only peace.

Everyone has a unique signature energy field which is called the Soul. You are not a body that has a Soul. You are a Soul who is generating a body and sustaining the body for the Soul experiences you are in this human dimension to learn and to offer your service and help others.

The Devil can be called the Lord of the physical. His sole purpose is to keep you attached to the illusion of the physical. When you cease generating and sustaining your human body, your body will cease cellular regeneration and become dust for recycling into new forms which appear physical.

There are two subjects on which I will now speak. One is Religion and another is Connection between External & Internal World.

Different Religions

Religion; There are many religions in this world that divide humanity. Some of the well known religions of the world are Baha'i, Buddhism, Christianity, Confucianism, Hinduism, Islam, Jainism, Judaism, Shinto, Sikhism, Taoism, and Zoroastrianism.

Hinduism as such is not a religion. It is the culture. However today it is popularly known as a religion.

Religions were introduced by Atmas at various levels to help humanity. We must remember that all Atmas (Sons of gods) came from only one source, that is God. Sons of Gods created through subdivision in various planes, developed different frequencies and wide ranging thoughts and ideas. In the process of subdivision they kept losing their awareness and power but kept on gaining wisdom, skills and vibrations. Some of these great Atmas or sons of Gods in different eras introduced the system of worship, preached to restore the path of righteousness, with common objectivity of uplifting the values in humanity and to create awareness of supreme power. Depending upon the part of the world in which they operated, language, culture, earlier practices also influenced the new system and the followers named their school of thoughts with a new name which became a *religion*.

Having understood that each religion on earth is brought with the awareness and wisdom by an Atma (call it a part of God or the son of God or a prophet or a messenger or a Guru) and the intention behind launching such movements is to make people understand the existence of God and pave the way to work towards building up of wisdom, skills and vibrations. Those Atmas also guided the people on right and wrong actions and advised them to take the right path.

Let us look at some of the aspects of a few religions known to us.

1. Hinduism: Maximum tolerance and flexibility exists in this school of thoughts. Wide ranging methods of worship and ways of life recommended. There are formal and well established methods of worship of God and on the other hand, you have the choice to worship in your own way. Call God by any name, or pray in any language, there is no bar. Though there is no organised management system established and in operation, Hinduism has thrived and prospered for millions of years.

2. Christianity: Based on principles of Judaism, Christianity prospered and spread across western countries as well as in other parts of the world rapidly. Sacrifices of Jesus Christ, son of god, and his ability to absorb the sufferings of his followers as well as his crucification attracted millions of people in the world. Christians follow their Sunday prayers in Church without fail. Well organised organisations set up by the followers worldwide and the movement popularised the religion.

3. Islam: Prophet Muhammad, one of the great Atma or a son of god, observed that people who followed the preachings by previous Prophets were not much involved. He realised that people have to be clearly told what they should do, what they should not do.

He was in contact with another great Atma Gabriel who guided him throughout. The Prophet wanted to bring various groups in the region under one umbrella. These groups were the followers of various past Prophets.

Prophet Muhammad was very specific in his preachings. He made sure that nothing was left to the followers' discretion or opinion. He clearly spelt out each and every essential principle of religion as below:

a God has to be addressed only as Allah .

b The Quran is the only holy book you have to worship now and nothing else.

c You have to pray only in Arabic which is Allah's language.

d You have to perform Namaz or Salat 5 times a day.

e You have to observe Ramadhan strictly.

f You have to perform Hajj.

Many other dos and don'ts have been clearly mentioned and strictly imposed. It is clear to Muslims that they can not ask any questions on what is written in the Quran. No deviations to what is written in the holy book is allowed. Prophet Muhammad made it clear that he is the last Prophet and the Quran is the only book they have to follow. The one who follows all points referred in the Quran, will be admitted to

Heaven on the day of Judgement which is considered a fundamental tenet of faith by all Muslims. If you fail to observe all the dos and don'ts mentioned in the Quran you as a sinner will go to Hell.

So a Muslim is compelled to follow all the instructions laid by the holy book Quran.

4. Buddhism: Buddhists believe that human life is a cycle of sufferings and rebirth, but that if one achieves a state of enlightenment (Nirvana), it is possible to escape this cycle forever. Siddhartha Gautam was the first one to reach this state of enlightenment and was, and is still today, known as the Buddha. Buddhism is a religion and philosophy that developed from the teachings of the Buddha (Sanskrit: "Awakened One"), a teacher who lived in northern India between the mid-6th and mid-4th centuries BCE (before the Common Era). Spreading from India to Central and Southeast Asia, China, Korea, and Japan, Buddhism has played a central role in the spiritual, cultural, and social life of Asia, and in the beginning of the 20th century, it spread to the West.

The *Lotus Sūtra* (Sanskrit: सद्धर्मपुण्डरीकसूत्रम्, romanized: Saddharma Puṇḍarīka Sūtram, lit. 'Sūtra on the White Lotus of the True Dharma')[1] is one of the most influential and venerated Buddhist Mahāyāna sūtras. It is the main scripture on which the Tiantai, Tendai, Cheontae, and Nichiren schools of Buddhism were established. It is also influential for other East Asian

Buddhist schools, such as Zen. According to the British Buddhologist Paul Williams, "For many Buddhists in East Asia since early times, the *Lotus Sūtra* contains the final teaching of Shakyamuni Buddha—complete and sufficient for salvation."[2] The American Buddhologist Donald S. Lopez Jr. writes that the *Lotus Sūtra* "is arguably the most famous of all Buddhist texts," presenting "a radical re-vision of both the Buddhist path and of the person of the Buddha."[3]

Two central teachings of the *Lotus Sūtra* have been very influential for Mahāyāna Buddhism. The first is the doctrine of the One Vehicle, which says that all Buddhist paths and practices lead to Buddhahood and so they are all merely "skillful means" of reaching Buddhahood. The second is the idea that the lifespan of the Buddha is immeasurable and therefore, he did not really pass on into final Nirvana (he only appeared to do so as *upāya*), but is still active, teaching the Dharma.

One Vehicle doctrine of Lotus Sutra is a revolutionary change brought in as a solution to serious complications encountered in the creation process of millions of years. This, if widely practiced, will end the misery and sufferings of millions of souls who will attain Nirvana, a permanent relief to births and rebirths.

It is time for people to start reading and following the Lotus Sutra.

5. Zoroastrianism: Parsis or Parsees are an ethno-religious group of the Indian subcontinent adhering to Zoroastrianism. They are descendents from Persians who migrated to Medieval India during and after the Arab conquest of Iran (part of the early Muslim conquests) in order to preserve their Zoroastrian identity. Prayers are primarily invocational, calling upon and celebrating Ahura Mazda and his good essence that runs through all things. Prayers are said facing the Sun, Fire or other source of light representing Ahura Mazda's divine light and energy. Purification is strongly emphasised in Zoroastrian rituals. Parsees are the most tolerant, most flexible in religious thoughts and practices and most important is that they are the most kind hearted people I came across. They sacrifice their needs and help the needy. They are very particular in attending fire temples for their weekly prayers.

If you study any religion, you will find all of them teaching about good things, dos and don'ts. In the course of time people down the line interpret the holy books to suit their convenience and this has caused severe disturbance and division amongst the masses on this earth.

This division is artificial and never existed in the beginning. Initially when the Gods descended, only they were there. There was no Shadow, there was no Emptiness. Some of the sons of Gods who had higher power created many Suns, Moons and Planets, some of them took the path to devotion and became His devotees. In this way many of the creations got connected to Gods and Devotions. When they got connected to these Gods, the process of reversal started. That means they wanted to merge with Gods with whom they were connected and retain their stability at the level of God in whom they had faith. Many failed in spite of worshipping out of their faith but they had no connection with God. This was not a good situation for them, because neither their behaviour or understanding of evolution was based on logic nor did they have connection to God for guidance. - In the absence of guidance from Gods, bad Karmas also got added. So they would do both wrong Karmas and right Karmas and continue with the cycle of deaths and rebirths.

Right Karmas are those which are connected with creation, with wisdom. Wrong Karmas are those which are of no use, like **desire, anger, greed, arrogance, infatuation and jealousy**. These souls, these creations when they die in physical life they will pass through the Lokas. There they will suffer in Hell and or be happy in Heaven depending upon their Karmas. This process causes loss of valuable time and also results in loss of the Cosmic energy that was used in the wrong Karmas as it gets dissolved or taken away by other sources. So the quantum of Karmas will decrease which goes on decreasing during the process of evolution because they were neither connected to God nor did they have wisdom to create. With the unending cycle of births and rebirths, if these souls reach the lower planes such as Planes 30 or 31, they will be left with only faith because they don't have adequate energy to apply logic and at lowest planes, faith is also not very easily available as connection to God is not easy.

Luckily for them Lotus Sutra had produced the Buddha System in the 26th Plane and in this plane, Buddha of the last Era had created Bodhisattvas. One of such prominent highly evolved entities was ALLAH. Gods could connect to souls even at lower levels and create connections directly through strong faith.

When a Muslim follows the dos and don'ts commanded in the Quran, performs Namaz by touching his forehead to Earth, he is connected to Allah. He is hundred percent sure about his faith. There are many Muslims who are not connected, they pretend to be Muslims. But many are true Muslims, they are connected to Allah, they perform their Namaz every day. They are truly connected because of the power of their faith.

Similarly people of other faiths who follow the preachings of their faiths would also be connected to their source, who may have different names but they all from the same source that is God. All depends upon the depth of your faith and good deeds you do in your life.

All these Souls will be saved. They will become part of the Shadow (Maya) and they will continue with the death and rebirth cycle or they will have a life in the next creation in plane 27. They will live perpetually. The Creation of which they are a part will be perpetual.

There are second type of people - They are logical, intelligent and know they are not connected to Gods and they will go on searching for answers and on the way they will try to understand through logic some good qualities of creativity i.e creation and go along with their life. Their negative energy is generated at a very low level so they also go through hell and after suffering and clearing Karmas they take repeated rebirths and in these births they again search for answers logically. It is these people who are in between. That means they are neither connected to Gods, nor do they have firm answers to their logic of the creation. We do not know where they will go, to any God who is easy to approach or whether they will take the path of Bodhisattva by coming in contact with Lotus Sutra.

Third type of people who in the era of Buddha, got connected to the Buddhas and Lotus Sutra. They have understood the logic of creation fully well and correctly. There are many avenues open to them. They can adopt brotherhood, sharing, helping, creating etc.

They have all positive energies and as they know what are negative energies, they avoid and shun them In this way they are stable, and growing and with connectivity with Lotus Sutra they also survive and prosper according to support they get from creation. So this is the whole process.

Future of Hindus is in between. Future of Muslims is firm. Future of Christians is also firm because Christ is another son of God who is capable of taking your negative karmas in the physical life itself without going through the Lokas. So all those human beings who are devotees of Christ, get an opportunity to clean themselves by a Confession to Christ if they are Connected and after they have Confessed they are clean to freely follow their path without going through the Lokas. This is their choice, they are lucky enough but they have to follow and completely abide by the principles of Christianity.

Regarding Hindus the majority of people in Kaliyug are in a state of flux. Many of them are logical, sensible people who have unknowingly adopted positive qualities and they try and shun negative qualities. They take rebirth repeatedly and search for the right answers. They are the ones who need to be helped by Lotus Sutra and ultimately by God's energies. Lot of Hindus and others who worship various Gods, will go back to their Source in the course of time. they will not exist. Their connection will become extremely remote. For e.g let us take the case of Lord Krishna. He has prominently got a lot of devotees on this Earth. His presence is felt even today by them. All those devotees of Krishna, will survive through Krishna and probably enter the next Plane of Existence i.e. 27th plane and 4th plane and continue the process further. If the Krishna Connection is available to them in the next plane, they will be lucky enough and probably again move higher but most of them will get disconnected, even if they are connected in this existing plane. They will again be in that state in which many Hindus are now in this Plane no. 26. Hope I am very clear.

To avoid such a situation where people with faith keep lingering in the cycle of death and rebirth, the only way out is to go for the 'Only one Vehicle' path of Lotus Sutra. Time is ripe to realise this long standing secret of millions of years of evolution of our Universe.

Connection between Internal world and External World.

I (Ram Peswani) am an ignoramus. I have been provided this Vehicle, i.e. my body to God at 5th Level and this God wants to convert the whole existence on this 26th level to a positive and beautiful creation, which is full of cooperation, sharing, wisdom and creativity and their existence is so smooth and so easy that diseases, death, pain of suffering, are all eliminated.

Following his supreme judgment, when God entered my soul at the age of 15 years, I had to overcome a lot of hurdles to connect with Plane no. 26 through the source of Inner world of this physical body.

It has taken from age of 15 years to the age of 80 years i.e. sixty five years to connect me to plane no. 26 through this source of Inner world of my physical body. I still do not know what is happening. I just tell what I hear and feel in the state of meditation. Now three very important souls came in connection with me.

One is my daughter Renu Peswani/Bathija. In spite of our wish and efforts to delay the birth of our fourth child, due to my wife's health condition at that time, she was born and she said, *"Look I am here, to come into the life of Ram Peswani."*

Why is Renu Peswani important? There are very few people who can see your Inner world. I am going through physical changes inside my body because of the Atma of 5th level. Renu Peswani is able to see to some extent and try to analyse, understand them and sometimes when she understands that little bit, she is also able to try to guide me by telling,

"Your energies are moving in this direction and this is the shape",

"I don't know what is happening further." To some extent she is also learning to see those energies inside the body and guide.

So first of all the book will play a very important role in the future. Through the book people of all types and religions, Hindus, Muslims, Christians, will come in contact. People with faith, people with logic, and people who are in between. So this book will be the source of external contact. When those people will come in contact there are three souls who are in contact with Ram Peswani. First is Renu Peswani, The second soul, he met forty years back is Guru Prasad. Now let us see what his talent is. He is totally logical and practical in his approach

He says *"I must have logical answers, I will not believe in anything blindly"*. He has no blind faith. He needs solid logical answers and he has the capacity to go on pursuing the logic, hammering his logic, till I reach the truth. This is what Guru Prasad is. Now what will be his role?

Many Souls will come in contact with this Lotus Sutra through the book. Lot of Hindus are in between. They are very flexible in religious matters but confused with a lot of things in life. They do not have satisfactory explanations on sufferings, dealth, rebirth etc. Most of them go on through blind faith because they don't understand or they are searching by logic or both. Here, is the person who will go on logically advancing the Science in the book, so that those people can get *sorted* out. *Look, I am a person of this logic or I am a person of faith. And if I am a person of faith, I might connect it or might not then let me again go back to connection or through logic.* So either they will get connected to Gods like, Krishna who really exists at present in this Plane and survive for the next Plane or by logic they will connect to Lotus Sutra and once they are connected to Lotus Sutra they know the right things to do, right actions , reducing their path of rebirths and going higher.

The third soul is Leena Prabhu, she is the editor of this book. She is reshaping this book and seems interested and gradually tuning to the way the book is shaping up.

In this world there will be numerous souls who will not come in direct contact with me.They will read the book and they will develop faith in the book and that faith will create a sort of Path for them and they will be guided by it. So 99% of humanity which will go through this book in future will get guidance through this book. This is because the internal world of Ram Peswani , Renu, Guru Prasad and the editor will give them more connections to each other, thereby work will go on.

Last Words

"For everyone who is born in the land of India has a natural spiritual inclination and is taught the basic principles of spiritual life; they merely need to be a little more educated in the Vedic principles"

~Vaniquotes[51]

They say "life is too short", yet long and worthy enough to look back at and put down on paper.

I have seen empires fade, governments dissolve, and people come and leave. I have witnessed the spiritual life of many sadhus, befriended them, and seen them exult in pure bliss and emanate a pleasant aura. My journey has been packed with extraordinary adventures and quests and has been a product of momentous decisions, such as my resolve to do business. One of the markers of a life well lived is surely the stories, experiences, and memories that are told, retold, remembered, and re-experienced throughout one's lifespan. Revisiting chapters from my

---

51Courtesy:

https://vanisource.org/wiki/CC_Adi_9.41_(1975)?hl=everyone|who|is|born|in|the|land|of|India|has|a|natural|Spiritual|inclination|and|is|taught|the|basic|principles|of|Spiritual|life long and eventful life in this book has allowed me to reflect on and relive them all over again.

The world tends to turn to youth for inspiration. But I would say, do not count out the grey-haired, for there are many things the world can still learn from them. It is the wisdom and skills I have accumulated over the years that have helped me reinvent myself in a meaningful way, for remembering invigorates my self-esteem at a time when I can no longer do the things that I once could do. As I stand today on the threshold of my ninth decade, I have attempted to retrace the steps that have brought me here, by channelizing my thoughts and recollections into this book.

As someone who has spent thirty years in meditation and learned countless valuable lessons that have continued to shape my life, I can ascertain that there is no better way to constructively contribute to the Universe than by serving Humanity and being AWARE. In my opinion, "Your own self-realization is the greatest service you can render to the world." as quoted by Sri Ramana Maharishi.

Do not indulge in rituals or religious practices, or even follow so-called spiritual masters of present times who supposedly advocate knowing everything about self-realization. As the earthly time frame for the physical body is limited, we just cannot while away our precious time in the infirmities of day-to-day life. Knowing well your selected path and self-realization mark the culmination of the indulgence in the welfare of the entire mankind all the time. Thinking good of all when we indulge in search of God, we realize that to become a pure soul or Atman we have to negate Karma to zero. To annihilate Karma, overpowering the five senses and mind forever is necessary. The whole journey of spirituality means lessening our desires and wishes in stages so that we can overpower the five senses and mind forever.

It is sincerely hoped that this book will pave the way for a new wave of interest among the youth and encourage and motivate them to don the spiritual garb and follow this path. Besides, all of us have an added responsibility to acknowledge and appreciate. Whether a man is on this path or has reached the goal, ask them questions and get to know them. They have carved and inherited a magnificent legacy of spiritual valor and dedication to serving Earth and mankind that can serve as a constant source of inspiration for the youth.

My story continues to be written. Despite retiring from the business thirty-six years ago. I have not allowed the pace of my life to slow down. My fitness routine and other interests keep me physically well and mentally stimulated.

It is sincerely hoped that the readers feel inspired to draw lessons from my life and find it well worth dwelling upon it today. I will continue to march upward and onward. I may one day sink into oblivion and fade away, but I am confident that will just be another beginning.

Until then, my dear readers,

engage in communion.

with your true inner self,

the Spirit existing in the heart.

~R. H. Peswani

Appendix

Contents

(Ref pg 2-Kalki Avatar)

(Courtesy: https://en.wikipedia.org/wiki/Kalki)

Kalki (Sanskrit: कल्कि), also called **Kalkin** or Karki,[1] is the prophesied tenth and final incarnation of the Hindu god Vishnu. He is described to appear in order to end the Kali Yuga, one of the four periods in the endless cycle of existence (*Krita*) in Vaishnava cosmology. The end of the Kali Yuga states this will usher in the new epoch of Satya Yuga in the cycle of existence, until the Mahapralaya (dissolution of the universe).[1][2]

Kalki is described in the Puranas as the avatar who rejuvenates existence by ending the darkest and destructive period to remove adharma (unrighteousness) and ushering in the Satya Yuga, while riding a white horse with a fiery sword.[2] The description and details of Kalki are different among various Puranas. Kalki is also found in Buddhist texts, for example the *Kalachakra-Tantra* of Tibetan Buddhism.[7][8][9]

The prophecy of the Kalki avatara is also told in Sikh texts.[10]

Etymology

The name Kalki is derived from *Kal*, which means "time" (Kali Yuga).[11] The original term may have been Karki (*white*, from the horse) which morphed into Kalki. This proposal is supported by two versions of *Mahabharata* manuscripts (e.g. the G3.6 manuscript) that have been found, where the Sanskrit verses name the incarnation to be karki.[1]

Hindu Texts

Kalki is an *avatara* of Vishnu. Avatara means "descent", and refers to a descent of the divine into the material realm of human existence. The Garuda Purana lists ten incarnations, with Kalki being the tenth.[12] He is described as the incarnation who appears at the end of the Kali Yuga. He ends the darkest,

degenerating, and chaotic stage of the Kali *Yuga* (Period) to remove adharma and ushers in the Satya Yuga, while riding a

white horse with a fiery sword.[2][13] He restarts a new cycle of time.[14] He is described as a Brahmin warrior in the Puranas.[2][13]

Statue of Kalki's incarnation on a wall of Rani Ki Vav (The Queen's Stepwell) at Patan, Gujarat, India

Kalki Purana

A minor text named Kalki Purana is a relatively recent text, likely composed in Bengal. Its dating floruit is the 18th-century.[15] Wendy Doniger dates the Kalki Mythology containing *Kalki Purana* to between 1500 and 1700 CE.[16]

In the *Kalki Purana,* Kalki is born into the family of Sumati and Vishnuyasha, in a village called Shambala, on the twelfth day

during the fortnight of the waxing moon.[17] At a young age, he is taught all the holy scriptures including about Dharma, Karma, Artha, Jñāna of the most ancient, the necessary wisdom of social320 perspective and military training under the care of the immortal Parashurama (the sixth incarnation of Vishnu).[18] Soon, Kalki worships Shiva, who gets pleased by the devotion and gives him gifts; a divine white horse named Devadatta (A manifestation Of Garuda), a sharp, powerful, strong sword, whose handle is bedecked with jewels and a parrot named Shuka, who is an all-knower; the past, the present and the future, while other gifts (armour, knowledge, powers etc.) are too given to him by other Devas, Devis, saints, and righteous kings.[19] Kalki then marries princess Padmavati (A reincarnation of Lakshmi), the daughter of King Vrihadratha and Queen Kaumudi of Simhala (the island of the lion) and princess Ramaa, the daughter of King Shashidhwaja and Queen Sushanta.[15][20] He fights an evil army and in many wars, ending evil, but does not end existence. Kalki returns to Sambhala, inaugurates a new *Yuga* for the good, and then goes to heaven.[15]

The Agni Purana describes Kalki's role:

Kalki, as the son of Viṣṇuyaśas, (and having) Yājñavalkya as the priest would destroy the non-Aryans, holding the astra and having a weapon. He would establish moral law in four-fold varṇas in the suitable manner. The people (would be) in the path of righteousness in all the stages of life.

The Devi Bhagavata Purana features the devas hailing Vishnu, invoking his Kalki avatara:

When almost all the persons in this world will turn out in future as Mleccas and when the wicked Kings will oppress them, right and left, Thou wilt then incarnate Thyself again as Kalki and redress all the grievances! We bow down to Thy Kalki Form! O Deva!

– *Devi Bhagavata Purana, Chapter 5*

Buddhist Texts[edit]

The central figure is a Yidam, a meditation deity. The 25 seated figures represent the 25 Kings Of Shambhala. The middle figure in the top row represents Tsongkhapa, who is in the top two middle rows. This comes from the scriptures that is part of the Indo-Tibetan Vajrayana Buddhist Tradition.

In the Buddhist Text *Kalachakra Tantra*, the righteous kings are called Kalki (Kalkin, lit. chieftain) living in Sambhala. There are many Kalki in this text, each fighting barbarism, persecution and chaos. The last Kalki is called "Rudra

Cakrin" and is predicted to end the chaos and degeneration by assembling a large army to eradicate a barbarian army.[7][8][22] A great war, which will include an army of both Hindus and Buddhists, will destroy the barbaric forces, states the text.[7][8][9] This is most likely borrowed from Hinduism to Buddhism

due to the arrival of Islamic kingdoms from the west to the east, mainly settled in West Tibet, Central Asia and the Indian Subcontinent.[23][24] According to Donald Lopez – a professor of Buddhist Studies, Kalki is predicted to start the new cycle of perfect era where "Buddhism will flourish, people will live long, happy lives and righteousness will reign supreme".[7] The text is significant in establishing the chronology of the Kalki idea to be from post-7th century, probably the 9th or 10th century.[25] Lopez states that the Buddhist text likely borrowed it from Hindu vedic texts.[7][8] Other scholars, such as Yijiu Jin, state that the text originated in Central Asia in the 10th-century, and Tibetan literature picked up a version of it in India around 1027 CE.[25]

Sikh Texts

The Kalki incarnation appears in the historic Sikh Texts, most notably in Dasam Granth, a text that is traditionally attributed to Guru Gobind Singh.[10][26] The *Chaubis Avatar* (24 incarnations) section mentions Sage Matsyanra describing the appearance of Vishnu incarnations to fight evil, greed, violence and ignorance. It includes Kalki as the twenty-fourth incarnation to lead the war between the forces of righteousness and unrighteousness, states Dhavan.[27]

Development

There is no mention of Kalki in the Vedic literature.[28][29] The epithet "Kalmallkinam", meaning "Brilliant Remover Of Darkness", is found in the Vedic Literature for Rudra (later Shiva), has been interpreted to be "Forerunner Of Kalki".

Kalki appears for the first time in the great war epic *Mahabharata*.[30] The mention of Kalki in the *Mahabharata* occurs only once, over the verses 3.188.85–3.189.6.[1] The Kalki incarnation is found in the Maha Puranas such as *Vishnu Purana*,[31] *Matsya Purana*, and *Bhagavata Purana*.[32][33] However, the details relating the

Kalki mythologies are divergent between the epic and the Puranas, as well as within the Puranas.

In the *Mahabharata*, according to Hiltebeitel, Kalki is an extension of the Parashurama incarnation legend, where a Brahmin warrior destroys Kshatriyas who were abusing their power to spread chaos, evil, and the persecution of the powerless. The epic character of Kalki restores dharma, restores justice in the world, but does not end the cycle of existence.The Kalkin section in the *Mahabharata* is present in the Markandeya section. There, states Luis Reimann, can "hardly be any doubt that the Markandeya section is a late addition to the epic. Making Yudhishthira ask a question about conditions at the end of Kali and the beginning of Krta – something far removed from his own situation – is merely a device for justifying the inclusion of this subject matter in the epic.

According to Cornelia Dimmitt, the "clear and tidy" systematization of Kalki and the remaining nine incarnations of Vishnu is not found in any of the Maha Puranas.[37] The coverage of Kalki in these Hindu texts is scant, in contrast to the legends of Matsya, Kurma, Varaha, Vamana, Narasimha, and Krishna, all of whom are repeatedly and extensively described. According to Dimmitt, this was likely because just like the concept

of the Buddha as a Vishnu Incarnation, the concept of Kalki was "somewhat in flux" when the major Puranas were being compiled.

This Kalki concept may have developed in the Hindu texts both as a reaction to the invasions of the Indian subcontinent by various armies over the centuries from its northwest, and the mythologies these invaders brought with them. Similarly, the Buddhist Literature dated to the late 1st millennium, a future Buddha Maitreya is depicted as Kalki. According to John Mitchiner, the Kalki concept was likely borrowed "in some measure from similar Jewish, Christian, Zoroastrian and other religions".[42] Mitchiner states that some Puranas such as the

Yuga Purana do not mention Kalki and offer a different cosmology than the other Puranas. The Yuga Purana mythologizes in greater details the post-Maurya era Indo-Greek and Saka era, while the Manvantara theme containing the Kalki idea is mythologized greater in other Puranas.[43][30] Luis Gonzales-Reimann concurs with Mitchiner, stating that the Yuga Purana does not mention Kalki.[44] In other texts such as the sections 2.36 and 2.37 of the Vayu Purana, states Reimann, it is not Kalkin who ends the Kali Yuga, but a different character named Pramiti.[45] Most historians, states Arvind Sharma, link the development of Kalki mythology in Hinduism to the suffering caused by foreign invasions.[46]

Predictions about Birth and Arrival

Kalki and Devadatta

In the Cyclic Concept Of Time (*Puranic Kalpa*), Kali Yuga is variously estimated to last between 400,000 and 432,000 years. In some Vaishnava texts, Kalki is forecasted to appear on a white horse on the day of *pralaya* to end *Kali Yuga*, to end the evil and wickedness, and to recreate the world anew along with A New Cycle Of Time (Yuga).

Kalki's description varies with manuscripts. Some state Kalki will be born to Awejsirdenee and Bishenjun,[47] others in the family of Sumati and Vishnuyasha.[49][50] In Buddhist manuscripts, Vishnuyasha is stated to be a prominent headman of the village called Shambhala. He will become the king, a "Turner Of The Wheel", and one who triumphs. He will eliminate all barbarians and robbers, end *adharma,* restart *dharma,* and save the good people. After that, humanity will be transformed and the golden age will begin state the Hindu manuscripts.

In the Kanchipuram temple, two relief Puranic panels depict Kalki, one relating to lunar (daughter-based) dynasty as mother of Kalki and another to solar (son-based) dynasty as father of Kalki.[49] In these panels, states D.D. Hudson, the story depicted is in terms of Kalki fighting and defeating asura Kali. He rides a white horse called Devadatta, ends evil, purifies everyone's minds and consciousness, and heralds the start of Satya Yuga.[49]

(Ref pg 7 -Infinity)

(Couresy:https://pparihar.com/2014/11/30/the-concept-of-infinity-in-sanatan-dharma/)

The Concept Of Infinity In Sanatan Dharma :

The Concept Of Infinity In Sanatan Dharma : God is infinite. But let us have a clear understanding of the meaning of this word infinite ; and use it in its proper sense. That which is not limited by time and space and not subject to the law of causation, which is above time, space, and beyond all laws is infinite. God is not limited by time or space, neither has He any cause. He is absolute. The infinite again must be one, otherwise it is finite. If there be any other thing beside that infinite then it is no longer infinite; it is limited by that object, consequently it has become finite. Thus if we admit that God is infinite, we deny the existence of any other thing besides God; other wise He would be limited by that

thing, and be subject to time, space and the law of causation. If we say that matter exists separate from and outside of God, we have made Him limited by matter, we have made Him finite and perishable. If we think of ourselves as separate from God, as independent of His Being, then in our thought we have denied His illimitable nature. There is for the same reason, not a single particle of matter in the universe that can exist independent of God s existence or outside of God. If He is infinite and one, our bodies and every thing of the universe from the minutest atom to the largest planetary system, from the lowest animalcule to the highest Being, exists in and through that Infinite Existence. This may be startling to many, but the fact cannot be denied. If we wish to be logical, if the word infinite conveys any meaning at all, we cannot avoid the logical conclusion which must inevitably follow. If, on the contrary, we use the word infinite meaning something finite, how foolish and illogical shall we be ! The conclusion is this : If God is infinite and one, then mind and matter, subject and object, creator and creation, and all relative dual existences are within that Being, and not outside of it. The whole universe is in God and God is in it; it is inseparable from God. I am in Him and He is in me; each one of us is inseparable from His being; if one atom of my body exists, that existence cannot be separated from His existence. Now we know that the universal Soul is infinite. How can infinity have parts? How can it be broken up, divided? It may be very poetic to say that I am a spark of the Infinite, but it is absurd to the thinking mind. What is meant by dividing Infinity?

Is it something material that you can part or separate it into pieces? Infinite can never be divided. If that were possible, it would be no more Infinite. Again, there can be no two infinites. If there be two infinites, how would you demarcate their respective spheres? (Objection): Why ? Space and Time are two infinite entities. (Reply): Space is infinite, but it passes our understanding how time can be infinite. Einstein's definition of Time is a gap between two sequential events in space, observed by an observer who does not change with time. Two simultaneous events define space and two sequential events define time. Vedanta defines time more subjectively, since 'subject' is included in the perception of time too. Time is the sequence of two experiences by the same experiencer who does not change with the experience. Each event-observation is counted as one experience. By bringing the experiencer and the mind associated with it to observe and record the experience, time is reduced to a concept in the mind.Time exists in mind. What is time?Time, for instance , means "succession," which is a condition of thought; and space means "coexistence." The activities of mind, being either in succession or simultaneous, produce the ideas of time and space; they are conditions, or, as Kant calls them, forms of thought. One thought following another gives us a conception of intervals which we call time. Time means succession in thought. When one thought rises after another, the interval between them is what we call Time, so it is subject to mental activity. When two ideas rise simultaneously, that which separates them is what we call space. Thus, that which exists between the idea " me " and the idea " sun " we classify as space ; yet it is purely a mental concept, having no existence outside the mind; for who knows any concrete thing designated space ? Hence, since these ideas of time and space are merely conditions of thought, they must be subject to change, because our thought is continually changing. Hence perception of time depends on the mind too. When there is no mind, or to put it more accurately when there are no thoughts, there is no time either. This is what we experience in the deep-sleep state, where sleep is considered as only one experience and not two. Hence there is no time or space in the deep-sleep state. They are valid as long as thoughts are there. The paradox of time arises strangely with the notions in the mind. Anything that is in space has form. Space itself has form. Either you are in space, or space is in you. The soul is beyond all space. Space is in the soul, not the soul in space. Form is confined to time and space and is bound by the law of causation. All time is in us, we are not in time. As the soul is not in time and space, all time and space are within the soul. The soul is therefore omnipresent. पूर्णमदः पूर्णमिदं पूर्णात्पुर्णमुदच्यते पूर्णश्य

पूर्णमादाय पूर्णमेवावशिष्यते ॥(Brihadaranyak Upanishad 5.1.1) This passage occurs in the Brihadaranyaka Upanishad. We recite it, chant it every day, but mostly we do not think about what it means when we chant it; it goes as a routine. Purna is fullness. The Upanishad says, "Purnam adah: that origin of all things is full; purnam idam: this entire creation that has come from that origin of all things is also full; purnat purnam udachyate: from that Full this Full has come; purnasya purnam adaya: having taken away this Full from that Full; purnam evavasisyate: the Full still remains unaffected." If we take something from something, the source is supposed to be diminished in its content to the extent

of that which has been taken away from it. This is common arithmetic. If we take something from something, the quantum of content in the original reservoir is lessened. If the world has come from God, some part of God must have gone to constitute this world and, to that extent, God must be less. Is it so? The Upanishad says it is not so. If we take away infinite from infinite, the Infinite is not reduced in any way, because one cannot take away anything from the Infinite. Therefore, if this so-called infinite of creation is taken to have emanated from that supreme Fullness of Infinity, it need not follow that there is some diminution of content in the original Fullness. After the emanation of this full universe from the full Origin, the Fullness still continues to be as it was, undiminished.

This is beyond our calculative method. We have never heard such a thing happening anywhere - that we carry away something and yet the source of that thing is as it is, without getting diminished. The reason is the character of Infinity itself. If some part of this finite is taken away, naturally it suffers a loss. If a limb of the body is taken away, to that extent the body has lost a part of itself. But you cannot take away a part of the soul. Here is the difference. You may take a part of your body, but a part of the soul cannot be removed, because the soul is not a substance. Therefore, it is not a finite thing. Therefore, it is not in any particular place. Therefore, something cannot be taken away from it. As we have our own soul, God is the Soul of the universe. This Soul is unlimited in its nature.The infinite character of God Almighty explains the reason why anything emanating from this infinite God cannot affect the infinite God. In fact, you cannot take away anything at all from the Infinite. The infinitude of God is not diminished in any way when the infinite universe proceeds, as it were, from God. Actually, nothing proceeds from God. Having done all things, He has done nothing.

The idea of proceeding arises only on account of the cause-and-effect relationship that has entered into our minds. Unless there is space and time, there cannot be cause and effect. Space and time are effects of creation and, therefore, cause and effect, having come after the manifestation of space and time, cannot affect Infinity, which is God. 1. First, would arise the concept of space, here vs. there, me taking up space over here, you taking up space over there. 2. Next would be time, if something is here and not there it has to get from here to there and can't be in both places at once, therefore, it takes time to travel from one place to another. 3. Finally causation, in space and time one thing seems to be the cause of another. In the relative sense all this is real. In the absolute sense none of it is real. So, you cannot apply the principle of cause and effect to God Himself. Therefore, creation is not an effect coming from God as a cause. Even the word 'cause' is not a proper term that may be applied to God. He is a causeless cause, no doubt, but He also is not a cause at all. The Infinite is spaceless and timeless; therefore, it is neither a cause nor an effect. Hence, when the full universe comes from the full Almighty, nothing has happened. It may look as if God has not created the universe at all, if we go deep into it. All the faults that we generally find with God for having created a bad world - ugliness, evil and sin - will be ruled out in one second if we realise that perhaps He has created nothing. He is exactly in the same glory that He was prior to that action that we are imputing to Him as creation. Having created, He is full. This universe also appears to be full for us in a relative sense. God is Absolute Fullness and the universe is relative fullness. "Om Shanti Shanti Shanti"

(Ref pg 11 - Ten Avatar of Lord Vishnu)

(Courtesy: https://i.pinimg.com/564x/96/89/c6/9689c61aa54a6f1e72c72b35c102cafa.jpg)

(Ref pg 12)

(Courtesy:
https://www.cs.ubc.ca/~goyal/creation.php)

Vedic Theory of Creation

Modern Science is unable to explain the process of creation as of now. The Big bang theory and Steady State theory have many loop holes and they do not appeal to everybody. Anyways, I will not discuss Modern theories of creation here. I am going to state what Vedas say about creation. Vedas are the sacred text of Hinduism, just like Bible for Christanity. Creation has many aspects, and it is not possible to talk about them in this article, so I will talk only about different phases of creation. Chapter 2.5 and 3.10 of *Srimada Bhagavatam* deals with the process of creation. Note that the *Puranas, Upanishads* are also considered as part of *Vedas,* besides 4 main *Vedas*. Before stating the theory, let me clear that English language does not have exact equivalents of the terms used in Vedic literature. So, I am using the terms and language used by other translations although the exact interpretation can be understood by reading the original text in Sanskrit, or in similar languages like Hindi. To understand them completely, please refer to Chapter 2.5 and 3.10 of *Srimada Bhagavatam*. From now on, I will use SB to refer *Srimada Bhagavatam,* and BG for *Bhagavata Gita.*

Here is the theory:

There are three basic material modes (qualities) of nature: mode of goodness (*Sattva*), mode of passion (*Rajah*) and mode of ignorance (*Tamah*). (SB 2.5.18)

There are nine phases in creation besides the one which naturally occurs due to the interaction of these three modes. In this article, we will mostly look into these nine phases. Eternal time is the primeval source of the interaction of the three modes of material nature. (SB 3.10.14, 3.10.11)

1. Of the nine creation, the first one is the creation of *Mahat-tattva* which is the result of incarnation of Supreme God (known as *Karanarnavasayi Visnu*). Then time is manifested. And in course of time, the three modes or qualities appear. Then, in the course of time, the three qualities interact resulting in further creation. (SB 2.5.22, 3.10.15). Note that time is created by Supreme God. So for him, everything (beginning, end) is occurring at the same moment.

2. Material activities are caused by *Mahat-tattva's* being agitated. Thus, in the 2nd phase of creation, the false-ego (*Aham*) is generated in which the material ingredients, material knowledge and material activities arise. (SB 2.5.23, 3.10.15)

3. The sense perceptions and elements are created in 3rd phase of creation. Here are the details:

a. From the darkness of false ego, the first of five elements, namely the sky (*nabhah*), is generated. Its subtle form is the quality of sound, exactly as

the seer is in relationship with the seen. b. In the course of eternal time, due to the transformation (reactions) in the sky, the air is generated with the quality of touch, and by previous succession the air is also full of sound.

c. In the course of eternal time, due to the

transformations in the air, the fire is generated, taking shape with the sense of touch and sound. d. In the course of time, due to the transformations in the fire, the water is generated, full of juice and taste. As previously, it also has form, touch and sound. e. In the course of time, due to the transformations in the water, the earth (solid) generated with the sense of odour. Thus, the qualities of sense perceptions are fully represented in earth.

So the transformation took place in the following order: ether (or sky) -> gas (air) -> fire -> liquid -> solid. (SB 2.5.25-29, 3.10.15, BG 10.8)

4. The fourth creation is the creation of knowledge and of working capacity. (SB 3.10.16) This can be understood as the laws of nature.

5. The 5th creation is that of controlling deities by the interaction of the mode of goodness, of which mind is the sum total. (SB 3.10.17)

6. The 6th creation is the ignorant darkness of the living entity, by which master acts as a fool. (SB 3.10.17)

Thus, after the creation of *Mahat-tattva,* time was manifested. Then 3 qualities of nature emerged in it. Then false ego was created. Then due to mode of ignorance, matter (5 fundamental elements) was created. Then its knowledge, and different activities of material knowledge come into play. In other words, the powers that evolve matter, the knowledge of material creations, and the intelligence that guides such materialistic activities were generated. Mind was created due to mode of goodness. Sense organs were created due to mode of passion.

When all these became assembled by force of energy of Supreme God, this universe came into being. All the above are natural creations by the "*maya*" of the Supreme Lord. Then a demi-god (*Brahma*) known as creator of the universe came into existence, who has the brain like that of Supreme Lord.

7. The 7th phase of creation is that of the immovable entities, like creepers, the trees with and without flowers, pipe plants etc. They are of 6 kinds. (SB 3.10.19)

8. The 8th phase of creation is that of lower species of life, like cow, goat, ass, mule jackal, tiger, birds etc. They are not intelligent species. (SB 3.10.21-25)

9. The 9th phase of creation is the creation of human beings. In the human race,

the mode of passion is very prominent. Humans are always busy in the midst of miserable life, but they think themselves happy in all respects. (SB 3.10.26)

10. The 10th creation, which naturally occurs due to the interaction of three modes are the creation of the demigods.

They are of eight varieties: (1) the demigods, (2) the forefathers, (3) the asuras, or demons, (4) the Gandharvas and Apsaras, or angels, (5) the Yaksas and

Raksasas, (6) the Siddhas, Caranas and Vidyadharas, (7) the Bhutas, Pretas and Pisacas, and (8) the superhuman beings, celestial singers, etc. All are created by *Brahma,* the creator of the universe. (SB 3.10.28-29)

Any theory of creation is incomplete without estimating the age, shape and size of universe. *Vedas* say that our universe is about 155.52 trillion human years old, and its total life span is 311.04 trillion human years (which is equivalent to 100 years of Brahma). In *Srimada Bhagwata* 5.20.38, the diameter of the universe is quoted as 500,000,000 yojanas (1 yojanas is equal to approx 9 miles, so its 4.5 trillion miles). The shape of the universe is egg shaped (brahmanda = brahma+anda). It may be interesting to observe that distance traveled by light in one day (186,000,000 * 3600 * 24 =~ 16 trillion miles) is equal to the perimeter of (vedic) universe (approximating ellipse to circle, perimeter of universe = 4,500,000,000 * 3.1416 =~ 14 trillion miles).

References: I have given references from *Srimada Bhagvatam* and *Bhagvata Gita*. Their online versions can be found at http://vedabase.net/sb/en and http://vedabase.net/bg/en.

(Ref pg 48 & 49)

(Courtesy: https://oneminddharma.com/what-is-metta/)

Metta Definition

Let's start with the word itself. Metta is a Pali word that is most often translated as "loving kindness." This is by far the most common translation of the term, but it's not our favorite definition of the term. Thanissaro Bhikkhu, a Buddhist monk & scholar in San Diego, is known for using the term "goodwill" as the appropriate translation. Thanissaro Bhikkhu makes the point that metta is not necessarily about a feeling of love, but more about wishing well for others. Although "goodwill" is a bit dry compared to "loving kindness," it may more accurately describe what metta is.

Gil Fronsdal, a teacher in Northern California, has been known to use the term "gentle friendliness," which is the translation we most often use. The Pali word metta shares roots with the words gentleness and friendliness, and the belief is that metta is actually a combination of these Pali terms.

Obviously we can't provide a single definitive metta defintion, but we find it to be a combination of both "gentle friendliness" and "goodwill." Metta is the quality of mind and heart in which we wish for others to be happy. This doesn't mean we are responsible for their happiness; rather, it is the wishing for the other person to be well and do what needs to be done to find such happiness.

To sum up what exactly metta is as concisely as possible, I'd say **metta is caring for the wellbeing of others and responding with a gentle and aware heart.** Metta is both a practice and a quality of the heart, and they're different (more on this in a bit). As a quality, metta is the state in which we see others as *l*iving and breathing beings and care for their happiness.

History of Metta

The practice of metta comes from the Karaniya Metta Sutta, which you can read by clicking the image. The metta sutta, or discourse, is believe to be the Buddha's words on this practice. It's a beautiful and short read (at least we think so). You can read it line by line and reflect on each statement individually.

Metta was not one of the practices that the Buddha originally taught his followers. According to Buddhist tradition, the Buddha sent a group of monks into a forest to practice for a few months. When the monks arrived, they found that the forest was haunted by all kinds of ghosts and tree Spirits. The monks ran back to the Buddha and told him of the experience. This is where the Buddha offered his monks the practice of metta, encouraging them to offer metta to these "evil" Spirits.

When the monks returned to the forest, they sat in metta meditation. They found that the Spirits stopped haunting them, and actually grew to protect the monks.

Now, this may be a true story or it may be an allegory. I wasn't there myself, so I cant' be sure. What I do know is that this is a beautiful example of how we can bring metta to difficult beings and situations that cause fear to arise in order to change our relationships to them.

In the 5th century CE in Sri Lanka, Buddhagosa wrote the Visuddhimagga. Widely considered the most important Buddhist text in Theravada Buddhism outside of the original Pali Canon, the Visuddhimagga gave us many teachings and practices. One of these is the way in which we often practice metta today, the repeated offering of phrases.

The Quality of Heart

Before we dive into the cultivation of metta through meditation practices, we have to understand the quality we are working to cultivate. There's so much we can say about metta and what it is as a quality of the heart, but we don't want to cause any overwhelm. As a heart quality, metta is a state in which we are present for beings. You can think of a time in which somebody has been a friend for you. Maybe they showed up when you needed support, maybe somebody held a door open for you, or perhaps a friend listened to you wholeheartedly when you were telling them something.

This is metta. It's important to recognize that it is not a quality we are trying to bring in from outside ourselves. We all have lived with metta in moments of our lives, whether or not we've directly practiced its cultivation in meditation. We all also know the warmth and contentment of having somebody else show up and be a friend to us. Metta is just that: the quality of the heart that allows us to show up with care for others.

Why is it Important?

Metta practice is important for many reasons, but there are a few that stand out. First, metta helps us cultivate a gentleness both in and out of our meditation practice. As we practice cultivating metta, we can bring it to our mindfulness practices and other meditations. We respond with less reactivity and more gentleness toward our own thoughts, emotions, and experiences.

It's wonderful to be able to bring awareness to our experience, but if we do so with judgement and reactivity we often are getting in our own way. Metta helps us in these mindfulness practices to tune into experience with some kindness and gentleness. In my experience, metta deeply impacts my level of awareness and insight. As I tune into experience with more gentleness, I am able to see it more clearly.

Metta of course helps us in daily life and our interactions with others as well. We respond with more care and attention to those around us, have more patience, and perhaps see others as living, feeling beings. This comes from cultivating

metta in meditation and from cultivating metta in daily life. After practicing consistently, we begin to see our relationships with others change, especially in our own responses.

Furthermore, metta practice is really a concentration practice, helping us to build the ability to focus. Instead of using the breath, we use the phrases of metta as the object of our concentration. Although it's a different way to practice, metta can lead us to deep states of concentration and ease in meditation.

According to the Mettanisamsa Sutta, the Buddha offered 11 benefits of metta practice:

1. *He sleeps in comfort.*

2. *He awakes in comfort.*

3. *He sees no evil dreams.*

4. *He is dear to human beings.*

5. *He is dear to non-human beings.*

6. *Devas (gods) protect him.*

7. *Fire, poison, and sword cannot touch him.*

8. *His mind can concentrate quickly.*

9. *His countenance is serene.*

10. *He dies without being confused in mind.*

11. *If he fails to attain arahantship (the highest sanctity) here and now, he will be reborn in the brahma-world*

(Ref pg 79) Supreme Path

Courtesy: http://cttbusa.org/lotus/lotus2_1.asp.html

Belief and Understanding

Chapter 4

At that time the wise and long-lived Subhuti, Mahakatyayana, Mahakashyapa, Mahamaudgalyayana, having heard from the Buddha, Dharma such as they had never heard before, the bestowal of the prediction of *anuttarasamyaksambodhi* upon Shariputra, felt it very rare.

They rose from their seats, jumped for joy, straightened their robes, bared their right shoulders, placed their right knees on the ground, single-mindedly put their palms together, inclined themselves respectfully, gazed at the honored countenance and spoke to the Buddha, saying,

"We, who dwell at the head of the Sangha and are advanced in years, told ourselves that we had already attained Nirvana and had no further responsibility, and we did not go forward to seek *anuttarasamyaksambodhi*." "The World Honored One has, from of old, been speaking the Dharma for a long time. Sitting here all this time, our bodies tired, we have merely been mindful of emptiness, signlessness, and wishlessness, taking no delight in the Bodhisattva Dharmas, in their spiritual penetrations of playfulness, in their purification of Buddhalands, or in their maturation of living beings.""What is the reason? The World Honored One has led us to escape the Three

Realms and attain certification to Nirvana. Besides, we are now advanced in years and when the Buddha taught the Bodhisattvas of *anuttarasamyaksambodhi* we did not give rise to even a single thought of longing for it.""Now, in the presence of the Buddha, having heard him bestow upon the Hearers the *anuttara samyak sambodhi* prediction, our hearts rejoice enthusiastically and we obtain what we never have had. We never thought that now we would suddenly be able to hear this rare Dharma. We rejoice profoundly, having gained great and good benefit.""It is as if, without our seeking them, limitless precious gems had come into our possession.""World Honored One, we would now like to speak a parable to clarify this principle."

"It is as if there were a person who, in his youth, left his father and ran away, dwelling long in another country, perhaps ten, twenty or even fifty years."

"As he grew older, he became poor and needy and ran about in the four directions in search of clothing and food. Gradually he wandered until he accidentally approached his native land."

"His father, from the first, had set out seeking his son but in vain. He settled midway in a city. His household was one of great wealth, with limitless wealth and jewels, gold, silver, lapis lazuli, coral, amber, crystal, pearls, and other jewels. His granaries and treasuries were overflowing, and he had many servants, ministers and assistants, as well as countless elephants, horses, carriages, cattle, and sheep. The profits from his trade extended to the other countries, and there were also many traders and merchants."

"Then the poor son, having wandered through various villages and passed through countries and cities, at last reached the city where his father had settled."

"The father had always been mindful of his son. Although they had been separated for over fifty years, he had never spoken of the matter to anyone, but merely pondered over it, his heart filled with regret, as he thought, 'I am old and decrepit. I have much wealth: gold, silver, and precious gems, granaries and storehouses filled to overflowing. Such a pity that I have no son! One day I'm bound to die, and when I do, my wealth will be scattered and lost, for I have no one to bequeath them to.' This is why he ever earnestly thought of his son. 'If I could only get my son back, I'd make him heir to my wealth. I'd be contented and happy and have no further worries.'"

"World Honored One, the poor son then, hiring himself as a laborer here and there, unexpectedly arrived at his father's house. Standing by the gate, he saw his father seated on a Lion-seat. His feet were resting on a jeweled footstool, and he was reverently surrounded by Brahmans, Kshatriyas, and laypeople. Necklaces of pearls, their value in the millions, adorned his body.

Attendants and servants, holding white whisks, waited on him right and left. Above him was a jeweled canopy hung with flowers and pennants. Fragrant water was sprinkled on the ground, and expensive flowers were scattered about. Precious objects were placed in rows, which were passed out and taken in on leaving and entering. Such were the adornments, and the majesty and authority of his awesome virtue.

When the poor son saw his father, possessed of such great power, he was immediately afraid and regretted having come there. Secretly he thought, 'This is perhaps a king, or one equal to a king. This is no place for me to hire myself out. I'd better go to a poor village where there will be room for me to work and where I can easily obtain clothing and food. If I stay here any longer, I may be forced to work.' And with this thought, he quickly ran off."

"Then the wealthy elder, seated on the Lion-seat, seeing his son, recognized him and his heart rejoiced greatly, as he thought, 'I now have someone to whom I can bequeath my wealth and treasuries. I have constantly been mindful of my son, but had no way of seeing him. Then, all of a sudden, he came on his own, and my wish has been fulfilled. Although I am old and decrepit I still longed for him with regret.'"

"He then sent attendants to follow him and bring him back. Thereupon, the servants quickly apprehended him. The poor son in alarm shouted in resentment, "I have committed no offense. Why have I been seized?" The servants, with even greater haste, grabbed him and dragged him back. The poor son thought to himself. 'I am blameless and yet have been imprisoned. This surely means that I will die,' and, even more frightened, he fainted and fell to the ground."

"The father saw his son from afar and said to the servant, "I do not need this person. Do not force him to come along. Sprinkle cold water on his face to bring him to, but do not speak further with him" Why was this? The father knew that his son's resolve and will were inferior and lowly, and that his own nobility was a source of difficulty to his son.

Therefore, although he was certain that this was his son, he expediently refrained from telling anyone, "This is my son." The servant said to the son, "I now set you free. You may go wherever you wish." The poor son was delighted, having gained what he had never had before.

He rose from the ground and went to a poor village to seek clothing and food.". "Then the elder, wishing to induce his son, set up an expedient and secretly sent two people, haggard and undignified in appearance, saying to them, "You may go there and gently speak to that poor one. Tell him there is a place for him to work here where he can earn twice as much. If he agrees, bring him back and put him to work. If he asks what he is to do, tell him, 'You are being hired to sweep out dung. We two will work along with you.'"

"Then the two servants sought out the poor son, and when they found him, they told him the above matter in detail."

"At that time the poor son first took his salary and then joined them in sweeping away the dung. When the father saw his son, he felt pity and amazement."

"Later, on another day, through a window, he saw his son at a distance, thin, haggard, soiled with dung, dirt, and filth."

"He then removed his necklace of beads, his soft upper garments, and his adornments and put on a coarse, worn out, and filthy robe, smeared himself with dirt and holding a dung shovel, looking frightful he addressed his workers, saying, "All of you, work hard! Do not be lax." By this device he draws near to his son, to whom he later says, "Hey, my boy! You should stay here and work. Don't go elsewhere. I will increase your wages. Whatever you need, be it pots, utensils, rice, flour, salt or vinegar or other such things, don't trouble yourself about it. I also have an old, worn-out servant you can have if you need him. So put your mind at rest. I am like your father, so have no more worries. Why? I am very old, and you are young and strong. Whenever you are working, you are never deceitful, remiss, angry, hateful, or grumbling. I have never seen you commit such evils as I have other workers. From now on you shall be just like my own son."

"Just then the elder gave him a name, calling him his son. The poor son, although delighted at this happening, still referred to himself as a lowly worker from outside. For this reason, for twenty years he was constantly kept at work sweeping away dung."
"After this, they trusted one another, and he came and went without difficulty. However, he still stayed in the same place as before."

"World Honored One: At that time, the elder grew sick and knew he would die before long. He said to the poor son, "I now possess much gold, silver, and jewels, and my granaries and storehouses are filled to overflowing. You should know in detail their quantities and the amounts to be received and given. Such are my thoughts, and you should understand what I mean. What is the reason? You and I are now no different. You should be even more careful that nothing be lost."

"At that time, the poor son, having received these instructions, took charge of all the goods, the gold, silver, and precious gems, as well as the granaries and storehouses, and yet he did not long for so much as a single meal. He continued to stay in the same place, still unable to let go of his lowly thoughts."

"After a short while, the father knew that his son had grown more relaxed, that he had accomplished the great resolve and despised his former state of mind. Knowing that his own end was near, he ordered his son to gather together all the relatives, kings, great ministers, Kshatriyas, and lay people. When they had all assembled, he spoke to them saying, "All of you gentlemen should know that this is my son, begotten by me. In a certain city, he left me and ran away to suffer desolation, poverty, and hardship for over fifty years. His original name was such and such, and my name was such. Long ago, in my native city, I anxiously sought him. Suddenly, here, I have found him again! This is really my son. I am really his father. All of my wealth now belongs to my son, and all that has been paid out and taken in is known by him."

"World Honored One, when the poor son heard what his father had said, he rejoiced greatly, having obtained what he had never had, and he thought, 'Originally, I had no thought to seek anything, and now this treasury has come to me of itself.'"

"World Honored One, the great and wealthy elder is the Thus Come One. We are all like the Buddha's sons."

"The Thus Come One always says that we are his sons."

"World Honored One, because of the three kinds of suffering, we have suffered much torment in the midst of births and deaths. Deluded and ignorant, we clung to petty dharmas."

"Today, the World Honored One has caused us to think about getting rid of the dung of frivolous discussions of the Dharma. We increased our vigor to earn one day's wage of Nirvana. Having attained this, our hearts rejoiced greatly, and we were content, saying to ourselves that, through our diligence and vigor, what we had gained in the Buddhadharma was plentiful."

"However, the World Honored One, knowing all along that our minds were attached to lowly desires and took delight in petty dharmas, let us go our own way and did not specify to us saying, 'You are all to have a share in the treasury of the Thus Come One's knowledge and vision.'"

"The World Honored One, using the power of expedient devices, has spoken of the Thus Come One's wisdom. Having gained from the Buddha the one day's wage of Nirvana, we took it to be a great attainment; we had no ambition to seek the Great Vehicle. Besides, the wisdom of the Thus Come One had been set forth for the sake of the Bodhisattvas, and so we held no expectations regarding it. What is the reason? The Buddha knew that our minds took delight in petty dharmas. He used the power of expedients to teach us in the appropriate manner, and we did not know that we were truly the Buddha's sons."

"Now we know that the World Honored One is by no means ungenerous with the Buddha's wisdom. Why? From of old, we truly have been the Buddha's sons, and yet we delighted only in petty dharmas. If we had thought to delight in the great, the Buddha would then have spoken for us the Great Vehicle Dharma. This Sutra speaks of only One Vehicle. In the past, in the presence of the Bodhisattvas, the Buddha had belittled the Hearers who delight in lesser dharmas, but he was actually employing the Great Vehicle in teaching and transforming them."

"Therefore, we say that originally we had not hoped for or sought anything, and yet now these great jewels of the Dharma King have come to us of themselves. That which the Buddha's sons should attain, we have already attained."

(Ref pg 87 & 120)

(Courtesy: https://www.accesstoinsight.org/lib/authors/gunaratana/wheel351.html#:~:text=twofold%20meaning%20of,of%20the%20fruits.

The Doctrinal Context of Jhana

The Buddha says that just as in the great ocean there is but one taste, the taste of salt, so in his doctrine and discipline there is but one taste, the taste of freedom. The taste of freedom that pervades the Buddha's teaching is the taste of spiritual freedom, which from the Buddhist perspective means freedom from suffering. In the process leading to deliverance

from suffering, meditation is the means of generating the inner awakening required for liberation. The methods of meditation taught in the Theravada Buddhist tradition are based on the Buddha's own experience, forged by him in the course of his own quest for enlightenment. They are designed to re-create in the disciple who practices them the same essential enlightenment that the Buddha himself attained when he sat beneath the Bodhi tree, the awakening to the Four Noble Truths.

The various subjects and methods of meditation expounded in the Theravada Buddhist scriptures — the Pali canon and its commentaries — divide into two inter-related systems. One is called the development of serenity *(samathabhavana),* the other the development of insight *(vipassanabhavana).* The former also goes under the name of development of concentration *(samadhibhavana),* the latter the development of wisdom *(paññabhavana).* The practice of serenity meditation aims at developing a calm, concentrated, unified mind as a means of experiencing inner peace and as a basis for wisdom. The practice of insight meditation aims at gaining a direct understanding of the real nature of phenomena. Of the two, the development of insight is regarded by Buddhism as the essential key to liberation, the direct antidote to the ignorance underlying bondage and suffering. Whereas serenity meditation is recognized as common to both Buddhist and non-Buddhist contemplative disciplines, insight meditation is held to be the unique discovery of the Buddha and an unparalleled feature of his path. However, because the growth of insight presupposes a certain degree of concentration, and serenity meditation helps to achieve this, the development of serenity also claims an incontestable place in the Buddhist meditative process. Together the two types of meditation work to make the mind a fit instrument for enlightenment. With his mind unified by means of the development of serenity, made sharp and bright by the development of insight, the meditator can proceed unobstructed to reach the end of suffering, Nibbana.

Pivotal to both systems of meditation, though belonging inherently to the side of serenity, is a set of meditative attainments called the *jhanas.* Though translators have offered various renderings of this word, ranging from the feeble "musing" to the misleading "trance" and the ambiguous "meditation," we prefer to leave the word untranslated and to let its meaning emerge from its contextual usages. From these it is clear that the jhanas are states of deep mental unification which result from the centering of the mind upon a single object with such power of attention that a total immersion in the object takes place. The early suttas speak of four jhanas, named simply after their numerical position in the series: the first jhana, the second jhana, the third jhana and the forth jhana. In the suttas the four repeatedly appear each described by a standard formula which we will examine later in detail.

The importance of the jhanas in the Buddhist path can readily be gauged from the frequency with which they are mentioned throughout the suttas. The jhanas figure prominently both in the Buddha's own experience and in his exhortation to disciples. In his childhood, while attending an annual plowing festival, the future Buddha spontaneously entered the first jhana. It was the memory of this childhood incident, many years later after his futile pursuit of austerities, that revealed to him the way to enlightenment during his period of deepest despondency (M.i, 246-47). After taking his seat beneath the Bodhi tree, the Buddha entered the four jhanas immediately before direction his mind to the threefold knowledge that issued in his enlightenment (M.i.247-49). Throughout his active career the four jhanas remained "his heavenly dwelling" (D.iii,220) to which he resorted in order to live happily here and now. His understanding of the corruption, purification and emergence in the jhanas and other meditative attainments is one of the Tathagata's ten powers which enable him to turn the matchless wheel of the Dhamma (M.i,70). Just before his passing away the Buddha entered the jhanas in direct and reverse order, and the passing away itself took place directly from the fourth jhana (D.ii,156).

The Buddha is constantly seen in the suttas encouraging his disciples to develop jhana. The four jhanas are invariably included in the complete course of training laid down for disciples.[1] They figure in the training as the discipline of higher consciousness *(adhicittasikkha),* right concentration *(sammasamadhi)* of the Noble Eightfold Path, and the faculty and power of concentration *(samadhindriya, samadhibala).* Though a vehicle of dry insight can be found, indications are that this path is not an easy one, lacking the aid of the powerful serenity available to the practitioner of jhana.

The way of the jhana attainer seems by comparison smoother and more pleasurable (A.ii,150-52). The Buddha even refers to the four jhanas figuratively as a kind of Nibbana: he calls them immediately visible Nibbana, factorial Nibbana, Nibbana here and now (A.iv,453-54).

(Ref pg 106)

(Courtesy:
https://en.wikipedia.org/wiki/Atma_Upanishad#:~:text=It%20is%20classified%20as%20a%20Samanya%20(general)%20and%20Vedantic%20Upanishad.&text=The%20Upanishad%20describes%20three%20types,(the%20Brahman%2C%20Purusha).

Atma Upanishad

From Wikipedia, the free encyclopedia

The ***Atma Upanishad*** (Sanskrit: आत्मा उपनिषत्), is one of the minor Upanishadic texts of Hinduism, written in Sanskrit language. It is one of the 31 Upanishads, associated with the *Atharvaveda*.[4] It is classified as a Samanya (general) and Vedantic Upanishad.[3][5]

The Upanishad describes three types of Self (*atman*): the *Bahya-atma* or external self (body), the *Antar-atma* or inner self (individual soul) and the *Param-atma* or highest

self (the Brahman, Purusha).[2][6] The text asserts that one must meditate, during Yoga, on the highest self as one's self that is partless, spotless, changeless, desireless, indescribable, all-penetrating.[7]

The text has also been referred to s ***Atmopanishad***.[8] In the Telugu language anthology of 108 Upanishads of the Muktika canon, narrated by Rama to Hanuman, it is listed at number 76.[9]

(Ref Pg 156)

(Courtesy: https://en.wikipedia.org/wiki/Nichiren_Buddhism)

Nichiren Buddhism

A bronze garden statue of Nichiren Daishon in in the Honnoji Temple of Nichiren Shu in Teramachi Street, Kyoto, Japan

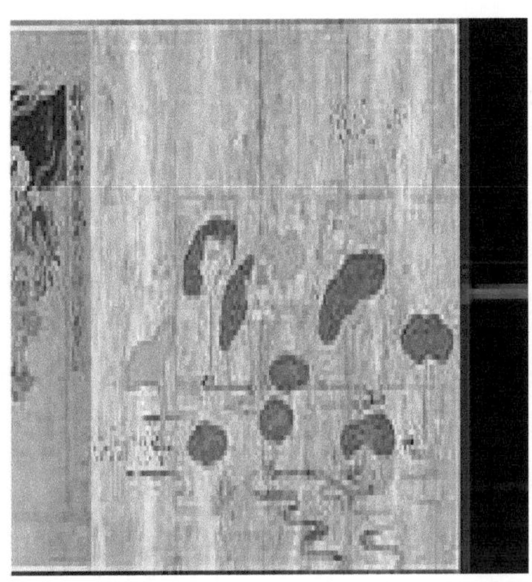

An illustrated image of the Lotus Sūtra, which is highly revered in Nichiren Buddhism. From the Kamakura period, circa 1257. Ink, color, and gold leaf on paper.

Nichiren Buddhism (Japanese: 日蓮仏教), also known as **Hokkeshū** (Japanese: 法華宗, meaning *Lotus Sect*) is a branch of Mahayana Buddhism based on the teachings of the 13th-century Japanese Buddhist priest Nichiren (1222–1282) and is one of the Kamakura Buddhism schools.[1]:239[2] Its teachings derive from some 300–400 extant letters and treatises either authored by or attributed to Nichiren.[3][4][5]

Nichiren Buddhism generally sources its basic doctrine from the Lotus Sutra claiming that all sentient beings possess an internal Buddha-nature capable to gain Buddhahood in current life existence. There are three essential aspects to Nichiren Buddhism:

1. The faith in Nichiren's Gohonzon

2. The chanting of Namu Myoho Renge Kyo with varying recitations of the Lotus Sutra
3. The study of Nichiren's scriptural writings, called *Gosho*.[6][7]:225

After his death, Nichiren left to both his senior disciples and lay followers the mandate to widely propagate the *Gohonzon* and chanting the Daimoku in order to secure the peace and prosperity of society.[8]:99

Traditionalist Nichiren Buddhist temple groups are commonly associated with Nichiren Shōshū and various Nichiren-shū schools. In addition, modern lay organizations not affiliated with temples such as Soka Gakkai, Kenshokai, Shoshinkai, Risshō Kōsei Kai, and Honmon Butsuryū-shū also exist while some Japanese new religions are Nichiren-inspired lay groups.[9]

The Soka Gakkai International is often called "the most prominent Japanese 'export' religion to draw significant numbers of non-Japanese converts", by which Nichiren Buddhism has spread throughout the world.[10]

Nichiren upheld the belief that the Lotus Sutra alone contains the highest degree of Buddhist teachings and proposed a classification system that ranks the quality of religions[11][12]:128 and various Nichiren schools can be either accommodating or vigorously opposed to any other forms of Buddhism or religious beliefs. Debate whether Nichiren's role as a Bodhisattvas of the Earth, a mortal saint, or an "Original Buddha" of the third age of Buddhism varies across its followers.[13][7][14][15] Nichiren Buddhism is practiced in many countries.[16] The largest groups are Soka Gakkai International, Nichiren Shu, and Nichiren Shōshū.[17]

9 789357 415583

Printed by Libri Plureos GmbH in Hamburg,
Germany